25

Bible
Plants and
Animals

Bible Plants and Animals

Volume 2

BIRDS AND OTHER ANIMALS

Harry J. Baerg

REVIEW AND HERALD® PUBLISHING ASSOCIATION
WASHINGTON, DC 20039-0555
HAGERSTOWN, MD 21740

The author assumes full responsibility for the accuracy of all
facts and quotations as cited in this book.

This book was
Edited by Gerald Wheeler
Cover design by Bill Kirstein
Cover Calligraphy by Aaron Presler
Type set: 11 pt. Clearface Regular

PRINTED IN U.S.A.

R&H Cataloging Service

Baerg, Harry J.
     Bible plants and animals.
     3 v.

     Vol. 1, Mammals. Vol. 2, Birds
and other animals. Vol. 3, Plants.

     1. Bible—Natural History.   I. Title.
II. Title: Mammals. III. Title: Birds
and other animals. IV. Title: Plants.

          220.85

Library of Congress Cataloging in Publication Data

Baerg, Harry J.
     Bible plants and animals: natural history of the Bible / Harry J. Baerg.
          p.   cm.
     Contents: v. 1. Mammals
     1. Animals in the Bible—Dictionaries. 2. Plants in the Bible—Dictionaries.
3. Bible—Dictionaries. I. Title.
BS663.B34   1989
220.8'574—dc20   89-32937
                                                                CIP

ISBN 0-8280-0499-4

Bible Birds

Palestine, though a small geographical region, is a crossroads for many of the migratory birds that pass through on their way from Europe to the tropical lands of Asia and Africa and back again. The Bible speaks of the seasonal appearances of the stork, turtle dove, crane, and swallow. They are still some of the most conspicuous of the migratory birds flying through the area.

The Scriptures mention only 35 species of birds by name (including the bat which the ancients numbered among them). Counting the migratory and resident birds, ornithologists have now observed 380 species in Israel. During Bible times also the region must have had at least that many. Biblical references to birds are spotty. The Scriptural writers refer to some of them often, but at the same time they entirely ignore large segments of bird life. Yet we must admit, however, that the Bible is still a much better source of information on the natural world than we find in any other literature of that time.

We will discover as we study them that, as with the mammals, Bible translators often puzzle as to which species of bird the Hebrew word has in mind. It is interesting to note that Scripture mentions most of the nocturnal birds known in Palestine today, including most of the owls.

A faint beginning of wildlife conservation appears in Deuteronomy 22:6, 7. Moses, giving instructions to the Israelites, considers the welfare of a nesting bird. "If a bird's nest chance to be before thee in the way in any tree or on the ground, whether they be young ones, or eggs, and the dam sitting upon the young, or upon the eggs, thou shalt not take the dam with the young: But thou shalt in any wise let the dam go, and take the young to thee." It was not wrong to take the young or eggs for food, but it was important to let the mother bird go to raise another family.

Another interesting observation is that all Bible writers, including the poets who authored the books of Job, Psalms, Song of Songs, and Isaiah; and who brought into their writings many images of beauty from the world of nature, that none of them speaks of the beauty of birds or mentions their songs. Only in a few instances does the Bible even allude to the voice of the birds. In Psalm 104:12 we read, "By them shall the fowls of heaven have their habitation, which sing among the branches." Ecclesiastes 12:4 states, "And the doors shall be shut in the streets, when the sound of the grinding is low, and he shall rise up at the voice of the bird, and all the daughters of musick shall be brought low." The bird in this instance was probably a rooster. Song of Solomon 2:12 declares that "the time of the singing of birds is come, and the voice of the turtle (dove) is heard in our land."

BIRD, LONELY—see Thrush, Blue Rock

BITTERN (qippod); *Botaurus stellaris.* L 30" W 50"

BITTERN, LITTLE; *Ixobrychus minutus*. L 14″ W 17″

Bible translators have really had a field day with the Hebrew word *qippod*. It appears in three texts (Isaiah 14:23; 34:11; Zephaniah 2:14), and the King James Version treats it as *bittern*. Other translators however, give us "hedgehog," "porcupine," "short-eared owl," "horned owl," "desert owl," and "ruffed bustard." Some of the renderings rest entirely on the derivation of the word without any regard to the context.

The first passage declares "I will also make it a possession for the bittern, and pools of water." The second reads "But the cormorant and the bittern shall possess it; the owl also and the raven shall dwell in it." The third reference says, "Both the cormorant and the bittern shall lodge in the upper lintels of it; their voice shall sing in the windows; desolation shall be in the thresholds." In reading the complete context of each text we find that both prophets are dealing with the retribution that will come on the kingdoms then at the height of their power. The reason for bringing *qippod*, the cormorant, the owl, and the raven into the picture was to show a place of utter desolation and ruin.

It hardly seems possible that the hedgehog or the porcupine would fit into either the first or the last text. Neither animal frequents pools of water, and both are strictly terrestrial, thus not likely to perch on ruined columns. Hedgehogs and porcupines would not sing or call from windows in the manner described by Zephaniah. Nor do they associate with the cormorant, raven, or owl.

The bittern is a marsh bird, a hermit that likes to live far from man. It does call at night with a booming, pumping, or stake-driving "woomph" that one can hear three miles away on a still night.

Both the bittern and the little bittern currently dwell in Palestine. Relatives of the herons, they are quite secretive, hiding in the marshes and feeding on fish and frogs there. When alarmed, the bittern straightens up, points its yellow bill up to the sky, compresses its slim body, and stands perfectly still. Its striped yellow and brown feathers and bill blend perfectly with the dry rushes around, and it becomes invisible.

Bitterns nest in the marshes about a foot or so above the water. When flushed they fly low with legs dangling and soon drop down into some other part of the marsh. They seldom roost in trees and are not likely to have perched on the lintels of desolate old columns as depicted by Zephaniah. It is quite possible that the prophets intended some species of owl when they used the word *qippod* to create the impression of utter desolation to which the kingdoms of Babylon and Assyria would succumb. We will refer to the word again under that category.

BUZZARD; *Buteo buteo.* L 21″ W 50″

BUZZARD, LONG-LEGGED (ra‘ah, nes); *Buteo rufinus.* L 25″ W 54″

The Bible speaks of the hawk only three times. The first two instances are in the Leviticus 11:16 and Deuteronomy 14:15 classifications of the unclean meats. The third (in Job 39:26, "Doth the hawk fly by thy wisdom, and stretch her wings toward the south?") refers to its powers of flight and migration habits. None of the instances cites a specific hawk. This should not surprise us, since we also lump many different species under the general term of hawk. In addition to the members of the eagle-hawk-vulture family that we have dealt with more specifically elsewhere, we will here mention the buzzards, harriers, and sparrow hawk, all of which were common in Palestine during the biblical period.

The buzzard hawks are the large, broad-winged, slow-flying hawks often seen soaring in the sky or perched on trees or telephone poles. The buzzard is closely related to our red-tailed hawk and the other members of the buteos in America. Since they are so visible, people have often accused them of being chicken hawks, and have shot them for that reason. Actually they live almost entirely on rodents and hares. It was probably a soaring buzzard that God had in mind in the passage from Job quoted above. We can distinguish the long-legged buzzard from the others because the adult male has a light, unmarked tail.

CHICKEN (Gr. ornis, alektor); *Gallus gallus.* L 25″

Common as chickens are in the Holy Land and surrounding countries, it is strange the Old Testament never talks about them. The only texts that may possibly refer to them are in 1 Kings 4:23 and Ecclesiastes 12:4. The first one lists the foods that constituted the provisions for one day for the tables of Solomon's household. The last item, "fatted fowl," could mean domestic poultry, but also wild birds kept in pens and fattened for slaughter. The harts, roebucks, and fallow deer listed previously were wild animals. The second reference, "He shall rise up at the voice of the bird," could refer to the crowing of a rooster. The word fowl appears frequently, but it refers to wild birds.

Naturalists believe that chickens, originally domesticated from the red jungle fowl of southern Asia about 3,000 to 5,000 years ago, and that the Chinese raised them in 1400 B.C. Just when they reached Palestine we do not know. It is possible that Solomon imported them with some of the other exotic birds and animals his ships brought in. On the other hand, they may not have been introduced until after the return from Babylonian captivity, or may have had only a limited use until a much later date.

BIRDS AND OTHER ANIMALS

The New Testament mentions domestic fowl in Mark 13:35 where Christ speaks of His second coming and warns His disciples to watch, for it may be at "even, or at midnight, or at the cockcrowing, or in the morning." The passage seems to make a distinction between the cock-crowing and the morning, which there is sometimes. The cock may crow long before morning. I have heard one crow a few minutes after midnight, though usually we hear cocks crow near sunrise. It may be such uncertainty that Christ emphasized.

When He sat with His disciples on the Mount of Olives overlooking Jerusalem, shortly before His crucifixion, He said regarding the city, "How often would I have gathered thy children together, even as a hen gathereth her chickens under her wings, and ye would not!" (Matthew 23:37). The picture of a protective mother hen is familiar to anyone who has lived on an old-fashioned farm. It must have been so to Christ. The clucking hen solicitously crouches with spread wings as the chicks run to her, find shelter under her, and then peek out between her feathers.

A rabbinical law forbade the raising of poultry in the city of Jerusalem, lest the scratching hens unearth some impurity that might defile the city. Nazareth, where Christ spent His boyhood, would not have had such a restriction. During the Roman occupation, which extended through Christ's time, the people must have ignored such a ridiculous ruling, for there were definitely chickens, or at least roosters, in the city, as our next texts indicate.

Probably the best known references to poultry in the Bible are the parallel passages of an incident in the life of Christ, of which Matthew 26:34, 69-74 is typical. Here the Gospel records the story of Christ foretelling Peter that he would deny Him three times before the cockcrowing the following morning. To Peter's great remorse, he did that very thing.

Crowing cocks, in spite of exceptions, were at that time, as they have been in many other places before and since, the alarm clocks that woke up the people of the city of Jerusalem. It was, of course, only an incidental use, for people then, as now, primarily raised poultry to produce meat and eggs.

CHOUGH; *Pyrrhocorax pyrrhocorax.* L 15"

Choughs, black, crowlike birds with relatively slender red bills and legs, share the communal trait. In the Holy Land they make their nests on seaside cliffs along the Mediterranean. They like to perform aerial acrobatics, taking advantage of the updrafts in the canyons, and seem to do it just for fun. Even sedate ravens sometimes indulge themselves in similar behavior.

COCK—see Chicken

COOT—see Moorhen

CORMORANT (qa'ath, shala, shalak); *Phalacrocorax carbo*. L 36″ W 60″

Two parallel passages, Leviticus 11:17 and Deuteronomy 14:17, refer to the cormorant as an unclean bird that the Israelites should not eat. In Isaiah 34:11 we read, "But the cormorant and the bittern shall possess it," and in Zephaniah 2:14, "Both the cormorant and the bittern shall lodge in the upper lintels of it; their voice shall sing in the windows." Both passages evoke a picture of desolation.

The cormorant could possibly fit the text in Isaiah, and it is quite possible that it would have perched on the lintels of ruined columns as described in Zephaniah, but the picture of it singing in the windows is a bit incongruous. It is essentially a silent bird, except that during the breeding season some have heard it utter guttural moans and groans. Later translations refer to *qa'ath* as either the horned, tawny, desert, or screech owls whose calls echo through the windows. "Owl" does seem to be a more plausible translation here than "cormorant."

The cormorant, however, does live in Palestine, both in fresh water and saltwater bodies. An awkward looking bird on land, it has feet that seem to be attached too far back. In water, however, it is an expert and graceful swimmer able to pursue and catch fish and eels with apparent ease. It grabs the fish crosswise in its sawlike bill, surfaces, turns the fish with a flip, and swallows it headfirst. This can be quite an undertaking when the fish is large. Cormorants are voracious feeders, and when the feeding is good, they will consume their own weight in a day. In some countries fishermen train them to catch fish for them from boats. The men tether them with a light cord fastened to a ring around the neck. The ring also prevents the bird from swallowing the fish.

Cormorants swim, using their large, paddlelike, webbed feet to propel them, and their folded tail acts as a rudder. They compress their wings against their sides to allow the streamlined body to slip through the water with as little resistance as possible. When resting they spend much time in drying their wings and preening their feathers.

Usually cormorants nest on rocky cliffs along the seacoast, but they may also build stick nests in trees on islands. In their nests they lay greenish-white eggs that are actually green on the inside as well. They usually congregate in rookeries or colonies.

Those who have tried to eat the cormorant's flesh feel that the prohibition against eating them was unnecessary since they smell and taste so much like rotten fish that one can hardly get the meat of a mature one down. The young are supposed to be edible only if skinned immediately, then wrapped and buried for a while.

CRANE (agur, sis, sus); *Megalornis grus.* L 44" W 80"

CRANE, DEMOISELLE; *Anthropoides virgo.* L 38″ W 70″

The crane enters the Bible only twice. In Isaiah 38:14 Hezekiah describes his delirium during his illness: "Like a crane or a swallow, so did I chatter." It could have been a reference to the calling of cranes during flight. Like honking geese the gregarious birds keep up a continual cronking as they fly. The purpose of the noise seems to be to keep the flock together on their long journeys.

The voice of the crane is remarkable, in that it comes through a greatly convoluted windpipe that, in older birds especially, may extend into the breastbone and flight muscles. As with the coiled tubes of a French horn the added length contributes greatly to the resonance of the call. In the case of the whooping crane such sound will carry as much as two miles.

The other Bible reference to the crane is in Jeremiah 8:7: "The turtle and the crane and the swallow observe the time of their coming." The passage alludes to the spring and fall migration of cranes. The common crane originally nested in a wide territory, including most of northern Europe and the Balkan countries. It migrated through Palestine to winter in Africa.

Cranes nest on the ground in swampy areas and usually lay only two large, olive-colored eggs with brown and black blotches on them. The weight of the young when they are hatched is only a fraction of that of the adults, but they are quite precocious and can run about almost as soon as they emerge from the shell. Their parents help them find plant and animal food that they eat voraciously and on which they grow and mature rapidly. They cannot fly until they are about 4 months old; then they must learn quickly to be ready for migration.

When migration time comes the cranes gather in large flocks, and after a few practice flights head south. They stop in certain areas to rest for night, not hidden in trees or bushes, but on wide, open banks where they can see all around. It is nearly impossible for either a man or a predator to approach without the whole flock becoming alarmed and rising into the air with a great clangor of calls and a confusion of flapping wings. At times cranes also fly at night. Then one hears their plaintive calls from the darkened skies as they travel unerringly along their routes.

In the daytime you can usually see them against the blue sky, neck and legs outstretched and broad, seven-foot wings slowly, steadily flapping. They soar only when landing. Cranes may assume an irregular V formation, but usually they gather in multiple, loose skeins across the sky. They have been known to travel as high as 13,000 feet, and one often can hear them above the clouds even when out of sight.

There are 14 species of cranes in the world, largest of which is the five-foot-tall, silver-gray sarus crane of Southeast Asia. Two species inhabit North America: the gray, sandhill crane and the large, white, whooping crane, that is now slowly recovering from near extinction. Two species also visit the Holy Land, both gray: the common crane and the demoiselle. The latter is smaller, has white plumes on the head, and black ones down the front. It nests in the marshes north of the Black and Caspian seas, and winters in Palestine and lands to the south.

Throughout the world the number of cranes has steadily dwindled, and the large flocks that once flapped across the skies in the Holy Land and elsewhere are no more. Several species are on the endangered list. They are long-lived birds but not very prolific. Even though they seem to do well in captivity, many of them seem destined for extinction in the wild.

CROW, CARRION; *Corvus corone.* L 18″
CROW, HOODED; *Corvus corone sardonius.* L 18″

The 19-inch carrion crow, Eurasian congener of the common crow of North America, abounds also in Palestine. One can distinguish it from the ravens by its square tail, smooth feathers, and its labored flight. Though its ordinary call is a "caw" or "haw," it can put a lot of variation, inflection, and urgency into its utterances, giving them a great number of meanings. The hooded crow, so called because of its black crown above a gray body, is a little smaller, but otherwise similar to the above. Some consider it a subspecies of the carrion crow. It too was common in the Holy Land.

CUCKOO; *Cuculus canorus.* L 13″

The Authorized Version has translated the Hebrew *shachaph* as cuckow in the two parallel passages on unclean meats, Leviticus 11:16 and Deuteronomy 14:15. Some doubt the choice of name, thinking it should have been sea gull instead. More recent translations are divided on it, but since two species of cuckoos do live in Palestine, we will briefly discuss them.

The common cuckoo of Europe inhabits the northern part of Palestine and the great spotted cuckoo dwells farther south. Most cuckoos lay their eggs in the nests of other birds and expect the hosts to hatch and raise their young for them. The cuckoo usually places its eggs in the nests of much smaller birds. When the chick hatches, the first thing it does is to push all other eggs or young out of the nest in order to get all the food. The young cuckoos are sometimes so much larger than their foster parents that in one case the mother had to stand on the youngster's head in order to feed it.

The great spotted cuckoo lays its eggs almost exclusively in the nests of members of the crow family. The disparity in the size of the young in this case is less, and the competition for food not as desperate. The head of the great spotted has a crest of gray erectile feathers crowning it. The creature is a rather noisy bird, and some have compared its call to that of a chicken cackling. Cuckoos are promiscuous in their mating habits, and the females may lay as many as 20 eggs in the nests of other birds. Usually the eggs resemble the color of the ones already there. To their credit, however, they are about the only birds that will eat hairy caterpillars, and in this way they compensate in some degree for their parasitic and antisocial nesting habits.

CUCKOO, GREAT SPOTTED (shachaph); *Clamator glandarius.* L 16″

DOVE, PALM (yonah) (peristera); *Streptopelia senegalensis*. L 10″

Several species of doves are native to the Holy Land in addition to the common rock dove that man has domesticated from earliest times. The latter has, of course, become feral as well and lives free in most of our cities, but it is also still found wild in Palestine. In speaking of doves we should first make plain that there is no scientific distinction between doves and pigeons. Local usage and tradition often apply the names interchangeably.

In the Bible the dove occupies the place among birds that the lamb does among mammals—it was the bird most often used as a sacrifice and the one that even the poorest individual could give. Mary, when she came to the Temple after the birth of Jesus, presented Him to the priest with a pair of turtledoves (Luke 2:24). Jesus Himself later, as recorded in Matthew 21:12, "overthrew the tables of the moneychangers, and the seats of those who sold doves" in the courtyard of the Temple.

Scripture often employs the dove symbolically. When John baptized Christ in the Jordan, the Spirit of God, as a dove, descended upon Him (Matthew 3:16). Jesus, when He sent His disciples out to teach, cautioned them to be "wise as serpents, and harmless as doves" (Matthew 10:16).

DOVE, RING; wood pigeon; *Columba palumbus.* L 16″

Noah, in the second mention of a bird in the Bible, dispatched a dove from the ark after he sent the raven. Twice it came back to him, the second time with an olive leaf in its beak. The third time it did not return, showing that the waters had dried considerably and that the passengers of the ark would soon all be able to leave it (Genesis 8:8-11).

The Song of Songs has much to say about doves: "Thou hast doves' eyes"; "O my dove"; "My love, my dove"; "My dove, my undefiled." Also we have the beautiful passage in chapter 2:11, 12: "For, lo, the winter is past, the rain is over, and gone; The flowers appear on the earth, the time of the singing of birds is come, and the voice of the turtle (dove) is heard in our land." The people of Bible times thought of the bird as representing conjugal love because they so often saw doves cooing to each other and courting. The mournful song of the turtle dove also represented sorrow. "I did mourn as a dove," Hezekiah said in Isaiah 38:14, describing his state during his severe illness.

One can pretty well recognize the many members of the dove family by their proportionately small heads, stout bodies, short necks, and nostrils that are thick and fleshy at the base. Their cooing is soft and often monotonous. The dove's thick feathers come out easily. When a falcon strikes a dove this fact may confuse the hawk and save the dove's life. Most doves are strong fliers and they appear to delight in traveling together as

DOVE, ROCK; *Columba livia.* L 13"

flocks. In Psalm 55:6 the psalmist sighs, "O that I had wings like a dove! for then I would fly away and be at rest." Tumblers and rollers are varieties of doves that have been specially bred to accentuate their penchant for aerial acrobatics.

Rock doves nest on the rocky cliffs along the Palestinian coast and around Lake Galilee. At times in the past they have multiplied to unbelievable numbers, flying in dense clouds in the canyons around the lake, or to the dovecotes in the villages. Isaiah 60:8 describes the future coming of the Gentiles to an enlightened Israel: "Who are these that fly as a cloud, and as doves to their windows'?" The windows were the openings to the nests inside the dovecotes. Such semidomesticated doves could be caught easily for the table when needed. The villagers would shoot those that nested on the cliff faces with arrows or net them.

All the villages and towns in Palestine had domesticated pigeons. Each homeowner had his dovecote, or hole in the wall, where the birds could live. Community dovecotes consisted of towers with many openings all around their upper portion and nesting boxes inside. They accommodated large numbers of pigeons. In today's civilization we find doves nesting on buildings and under bridges. Their nests are rather sketchy, consisting of a few twigs. In each nest the female lays 2 white eggs.

When the young hatch, they receive "pigeon's milk," a milky, cheese-like secretion of the crop lining of both parents during the nesting period.

DOVE, STOCK; *Columba oenas.* L 13"

The adult birds transfer it to the open bill of the young, and the nestlings grow rapidly on it. Soon the parents add berries, partly digested weed seeds, and grain. The people of the Middle East often take the birds from the nest just before they are ready to fly and prepare them as a choice table delicacy, fat and tender.

The story of the famine in Samaria (2 Kings 6:25-30) emphasizes the extreme hunger of the besieged. Food was so scarce that "the fourth part of a cab of dove's dung [sold] for five pieces of silver." Some commentators say, however (and it sounds reasonable), that it was not the dung, but the contents of the pigeon's crops, the mix of pigeon's milk and grains, that the people bought. This was a food that even the armies of the besiegers could not keep out, and it was probably quite nourishing.

Geneticists tell us that man has bred all of our domestic pigeons, in all their varied colors and forms, from the original domesticated rock doves. This includes the tumblers, rollers, pouters, fantails, and Jacobins, as well as those bred for eating, racing, and homing.

Mankind has long recognized the ability of pigeons to find their way home from great distances and has used it to his advantage. Caesar, when fighting his campaigns in Gaul, sent back home, by carrier pigeon, messages of his conquests. Wellington, after the Battle of Waterloo, dispatched word of his success to England by pigeons and it got there four days ahead of couriers by horse and boat. During World War I the Lost Battalion of Major Charles Whittelsey in the Argonne Forest saved itself

DOVE, TURTLE (tor) (trugon); *Streptopelia turtur.* L 11″
DOVE, COLLARED TURTLE; *Streptopelia decaocto.* L 11″

when, after all other means had failed, he managed to get a message for help through heavy fire by the noted war pigeon, Cher Ami.

How homing pigeons find their way, sometimes through fog at sea, science does not yet fully understand. Evidently they use more than one clue. In today's world of electronic communication we no longer need pigeons for sending messages, but a number of breeders of carrier pigeons still find it rewarding to raise and race them as a hobby.

The wood pigeon, or ring dove, is the largest of the European doves. One can recognize it by a partial white collar and large white wing patches. It usually nests in trees. The stock dove is smaller and lacks the white patches. The turtledoves, sometimes just called turtles in the Bible, are much smaller, more like our mourning dove or the extinct passenger pigeon whose vast numbers once darkened the skies of our Eastern states. The turtle dove's tail, however, is not long and pointed. The collared turtle dove's persistent "coo-coo" is probably the Bible's "song of the turtle." The palm dove is another small dove that lives in Palestine. Even now one often sees it in towns and villages, and it nests in palm trees.

EAGLE, BONELLI'S; *Hieratus fasciatus*. L 28" W 64"
EAGLE, GIER—see Vulture, Egyptian; Vulture, Griffon

The Hebrew terms *nesher* and *asniyeh*, as used in the Bible, usually denote the eagle. At times translators have rendered them as vulture, but in most instances, as in the following texts, the eagle is the bird that the original author had in mind: the parallel texts in Leviticus 11:13 and Deuteronomy 14:12 that refer to it as being unclean; Deuteronomy 28:49, Job 9:26, and Proverbs 23:5 speak of the swift flight of the eagle; and Ezekiel 1:10; 17:3, 7; Daniel 7:4; and others employ it symbolically in prophecies.

Young eagles, when nearly full grown, weigh even more than their parents, but they are fat and flabby, not in the best condition for flying. The parents then begin an exercising program for them. They stand on the edge of the nest and flap their wings, encouraging the young to imitate them. The eagles then do a lot of flapping, but that still does not give them skill in flying. When they are ready to leave the nest, the mother will tempt them with some food a short distance away. They try to fly, become confused, and start to fall. The mother swoops down under the falling youngster and carries it on her back till it catches the air under its wings again. Then the mother drops out from under it and gives it another chance. In this way the young slowly learn to fly.

Moses must have watched this happen as he herded sheep in the desert. He refers to it in his song in Deuteronomy 32:11, showing how the Lord

EAGLE, GOLDEN (nesher, neshar, asniyeh) (aetos); *Aquila chrysaetos.* L 33" W 74"

patiently led His people, "as an eagle stirreth up her nest, fluttereth over her young, spreadeth abroad her wings, taketh them, beareth them on her wings."

In Isaiah 40:31 we read, "They that wait upon the Lord shall renew their strength. They shall mount up with wings as eagles." And in Psalm 103:5: ". . . so that thy youth is renewed like the eagle's." The passages seem to point to a partial eclipse of the eagle's power during molting. Then, as the new feathers grow out, the eagle's strength renews itself, and it can soar again in the sky as it has in the past.

At least four species of eagles have lived in the Holy Land in the past, and most of them still do. Bonelli's eagle, one of the smaller ones, is brown above and lighter below. The forward parts of the wings are dark, and the tail has a dark band across the end. It is still fairly common in Palestine.

Chief among these big birds is the golden eagle which ranges over most of the Northern Hemisphere. It is a large bird. The females are about 33 inches tall with a wingspread of more than six feet, while the males, as with others of the hawk family, are smaller. In its adult plumage it is dark brown all over except for the feathers of the head and back of the neck, which are tipped with a tawny gold color. The strong, heavily clawed feet

EAGLE, IMPERIAL; *Aquila heliaca.* L 32" W 73"

strike its prey or grasp it. Though like other predatory birds it lives by preying on other animals and birds, it is not necessarily cruel. It kills them by a sudden blow, usually from behind, or quickly crushes out the life with its sharp talons. The diet of the Palestinian golden eagle is mostly hares, hyraxes, rodents, young game animals, and larger game birds. The creature is rare in Palestine now. A bird of the mountains and open plains, it nests on lofty crags. Because eagles use their nests year after year, they build the nests up with an accumulation of sticks that sometimes get so large it would take a three-ton truck to move them. Golden eagles stake out a territory that may be 20 to 60 square miles in area. This makes it a solitary bird, not inclined to gather in flocks as do the vultures.

Another species fairly common in Palestine even now is the imperial eagle. Like the golden eagle, it is also a large bird with tawny feathers on the head and neck, but it differs from the latter in having white shoulder patches. A bird of the forests, it occupies the coastal mountains that receive more rainfall than do those of the interior. Because it lives in the forest, people do not see it as often as some of the other eagles.

Most common of all the eagles in Palestine now is the short-toed eagle. Its population has not declined as much as the others have by the

EAGLE, SHORT-TOED; *Circaetus gallicus.* L 27" W 62"

poisoning of rodents, because it lives largely on reptiles and frogs. Each pair chooses a valley and hunts regularly up and down its rocky slopes. When it detects prey it hovers briefly, then, closing its wings, it dives to capture its victim. Short-toed eagles kill many poisonous snakes. The smallest of the four species, it is not much more than two feet tall, with a wingspread of little more than five feet, about the size of a large hawk. In color it is grayish brown above, lighter below with black wing tips and barred tail.

The Arabs used some eagles, especially the golden, in falconry to hunt deer, antelope, and the larger game birds. In the Bible, however, we find no mention of falconry, and we must assume that the Hebrews did not engage in that sport.

EGRET—see Heron

The graceful little egret has pure white feathers with beautiful head plumes and erectile, lacy egrets on its back during the summer. We can always distinguish it from the other white herons and egrets by its "bare" feet—yellow on black legs. The much larger great white heron lacks the plumes on the head and has black feet and legs.

EGRET, CATTLE; *Ardeola ibis.* L 20″ W 37″

EGRET, LITTLE; *Egretta garzetta.* L 24″ W 38″

FALCON, LANNER (ra'ah, dayah) *Falco lanarius.* L 17" W 39"
FALCON, RED-FOOTED; *Falco verspertinus.* L 11" W 25"
FALCON, SAKER; *Falco cherrug.* L 18" W 41"
  HOBBY; *Falco subbuteo.* L 11" W 28"
  KESTREL; *Falco tinnunculus.* L 12" W 28"
  KESTREL, LESSER; *Falco naumanni.* L 11" W 25"
  MERLIN; *Falco columbarius.* L 11" W 25"

Translators question the Hebrew word *ra'ah* translated as "glede" in Deuteronomy 14:13 of the KJV. Some believe that it should have been *dayah* as in the parallel passage in Leviticus 11:14. However, the word *raah* means vision, or keen eyesight, and could well apply to most hawks and vultures. A number think it refers to the falcons, buzzard hawks, or kites.

Among falcons, the most important one in the Holy Land would be the peregrine. It is the same one known by that name and also as the duck hawk in America. The peregrine often lives and nests on rocky seashores and finds its prey among the shore birds, ducks, and pigeons that abound there. Usually it sits still on a boulder and observes the movement of wildlife within the range of its keen vision. When it sees potential prey, it flies quickly in that direction. Approaching from above, it dives with its

FALCON, PEREGRINE; *Falco peregrinus*. L 18″ W 40″

long, pointed wings folded, at speeds of up to 160 miles per hour. With its closed "fists" it strikes and usually kills instantly, retrieving its prey as it falls to the ground. Sometimes it will strike out with open talons and pick off a smaller bird out of the air as it passes.

The peregrine was the royal falcon and thus reserved for kings in the sport of falconry that flourished during the Middle Ages. Men trained the falcons to kill birds and foxes, and to point out wolves and deer for the hunters on horseback.

The lanner falcon, a slightly smaller bird that also dwells in Palestine, has a more easterly distribution. In appearance it resembles our prairie falcon and, like it, prefers to live farther inland, feeding on the flocks of doves that were common during Bible times. The similar but still lighter colored saker falcon inhabits the desert regions of Palestine. Other smaller falcons sometimes seen there are the hobby, red-footed falcon, merlin, and the two kestrels. Most of them just pass through there on the way to their wintering grounds in Africa.

31

GULL, BLACK-HEADED; *Larus ridibundus*, L 14″
GULL, COMMON; *Larus canus*. L 16″

GULL, HERRING (shachaph); *Larus argentatus*. L 22″

The New International Version of the Bible, and possibly others, translates the Hebrew word *shachaph* in the Levitical diet restrictions as "gull." Without doubt gulls inhabited Palestine during Bible times as well as now, so we can at least mention them. Two of the larger species you will likely see there are the wide-ranging herring gull and the lesser black-backed gull. Both frequent the seacoasts and the inland seas. Among the medium-sized gulls we find the common and the slender-billed gull. Each is a gray-mantled, white-headed, white-tailed bird. The common has black wing tips with white spots on the tips of the primaries, while the slender-billed has white leading edges and black along the tips of the primaries. It also has a red bill and legs.

Three black-backed gulls have widespread ranges: the Mediterranean, with white wing tips and tail; the black-headed, with white leading edges, but black tips on the primaries; and the little gull, recognized not only by its size but also its gray wings with white tips. These gulls often come inland and follow the plowman in the fields.

It seems a shame that Scripture speaks of this bird only to classify it as unclean and not to be eaten. Gulls are marvelous fliers and mostly scavenge marine life. They will drop seashells from the air onto boulders to crack them open.

GULL, LESSER BLACK-BACKED; *Larus fuscus.* L 21"
GULL, LITTLE; *Larus minutus.* L 11"

GULL, MEDITERRANEAN; *Larus melanocephalus.* L 15"
GULL, SLENDER-BILLED; *Larus genei.* L 17"
GALLINULE—see Moorhen
GLEDE—see Kite; Hawk
HARRIER, HEN; *Circus cyaneus.* L 18" W 41"

HARRIER, MARSH; *Circus aeruginosus.* L 21″ W 46″
HARRIER, PALLID; *Circus macrourus.* L 17″ W 40″

The three harriers found in Palestine are similar to our northern harrier in that they are slim, long-winged hawks that usually fly low over marshes and meadows, and the adult males usually show white upper tail coverts. The birds nest on the ground in marshes and perch on hummocks or stubs. Harriers feed largely on mice, frogs, salamanders, and the young of marsh birds. They have received the name harriers because of the way they quarter back and forth over their hunting area to make sure that they have missed nothing.

The male marsh harrier is brown with gray wings and an unbarred tail. The hen harrier looks much like the American northern harrier. The female has brown feathers with a barred tail and prominent, white upper tail coverts. The gray male has black wing tips. The male pallid harrier is gray, has no white rump patch, but a white head and under parts, and a lightly barred tail.

HAWK, HOBBY—see Falcon

HAWK, SPARROW (nes); *Accipitor nisus.* L 14″ W 29″

The sparrow hawk of Europe is not the same as the one that formerly went by that name here until recently changed to American kestrel. The Old World sparrow hawk is an accipiter, similar to our sharp-shinned hawk, and closely related to the Cooper's hawk and goshawk. The sparrow hawks which live and nest in the woods or on rocky cliffs, subsist largely on small birds, rodents, and insects, especially dragonflies, many of which they catch on the wing. With their rounded wings and long tails, they are expert at maneuvering and well able to follow dodging prey. These hawks will make off with baby chickens if they get a chance, and they are the ones that deserve the name of "chicken hawk" rather than the highly visible buteos.

HERON, GOLIATH; *Ardea goliath.* L 54"

Leviticus 11:19 and Deuteronomy 14:18, the only two references to the heron, both times present the bird as unfit for food to the Israelites. At present 10 birds found in Palestine fit that loose classification. Some, like the bitterns, we have already dealt with. Prominent among the others is the gray heron, the European equivalent of the great blue heron of America. When the gray heron flies, it slowly flaps its large wings and takes off with its long neck folded back into an S curve. This characteristic always distinguishes the herons and egrets from the cranes, which fly like geese, with their necks outstretched.

Some fishermen are antagonistic to this fellow fisherman, but studies show that human beings have little reason to feel hostile toward herons. Herons take mostly the small fry or the trash fish that need to be thinned out anyway to leave more room for the game fish. In unprotected fish hatcheries they can, however, be quite destructive.

The large herons inhabit both fresh and salt marshes, along streams, and even pastures. They are alert to danger and take off with a resonant "squaak" when someone approaches too near.

The goliath heron, largest of them all, is up to five feet tall, otherwise similar to the gray. It lives in Asia, but sometimes visits Palestine. A

HERON, GREAT WHITE; *Egretta alba.* L 35" W 55"

smaller species, the purple heron, resembles our Louisiana heron, but its body is reddish. It is more active than the larger birds when feeding.

The black-crowned herons—blue-gray, white, and black—are smaller

HERON, GRAY (anaphah); *Ardea cinerea.* L 36″ W 55″

HERON, NIGHT; *Nycticorax nycticorax.* L 24″ W 44″

37

and have shorter necks and legs. They come to the feeding grounds toward evening and leave in the morning when the day shift arrives.

The squacco herons and the cattle egrets have bodies similar to the night herons, but they are almost white birds. The latter have earned their name because of their habit of feeding around cattle. They catch the insects disturbed by the grazing animals. Often the birds will perch on the backs of the cattle. They have buffy feathers on their backs and fronts during the breeding season. The squacco heron has more buff color than the cattle egret and, like the night heron, is more of a night feeder.

Herons and egrets like to nest in mixed colonies. Although their nests may crowd each other, they seem to get along without too many territorial disputes. Usually they nest in trees on islands, but in Israel and some other places they occupy papyrus swamps also. Papyrus plants grow tall and sturdy in water that may be too thick to row in.

HERON, PURPLE; *Ardea purpurea.* L 31" W 45"

HERON, SQUACCO; *Ardeola ralloides.* L 18" W 34"

HOBBY—see Falcon

HOOPOE (dukiphath); *Upupa epops.* L 11″

Most commentators agree that the Hebrew word *dukiphath,* used only in the parallel passages in Leviticus 11:19 and Deuteronomy 14:18 to discuss unclean meats, should have been translated "hoopoe" instead of "lapwing," as it is in the KJV. It is so rendered in most of the modern versions.

Some believe that the prohibition against eating the flesh of the hoopoe may be due, at least in part, to the unsanitary condition of their nests, usually made in tree cavities. The parent birds never remove the young bird's droppings, as most other birds do, and as a result the nests have a rather foul odor. In addition, the females, during nesting, have an active preening gland above the base of the tail from which they can actually spray a strongly musky, dark-brown liquid as a repellant, should an enemy be so rash as to want to disturb the occupants of the nest. The birds seem to depend quite heavily upon this deterrent, and can be caught by hand then if one can stand the smell.

The eggs hatch in about two weeks, but the adults must feed their naked young for nearly a month before they are ready to leave. The female does all the brooding and caring for the young, but the male feeds her on the nest, and relays food through her to the young. He does not, however, seal her into the nesting cavity as does the related hornbill. Hoopoes are in a small family by themselves, together with the wood hoopoes, and live mostly in Asia and Africa. For the breeding season they migrate north to Palestine and southern Europe.

One can easily recognize and remember these strikingly marked birds by their large, erectile crests of black and white tipped, light cinnamon feathers, which they keep raising and lowering and also by their black-and-white barred wing and tail feathers. The birds are not at all retiring, but often appear in the open on lawns or in parks, and they seem to be quite tame and fearless. They prefer running to flying when approached. When they do fly, they go with an undulating flight like that of the woodpeckers.

As an insect feeder, the hoopoe devours many worms, caterpillars, crickets, and grasshoppers. It is especially fond of the grubs of wood-boring beetles, which it digs out of rotten logs with its long, slim, curved bill.

The call of the hoopoe is a far-carrying "hoo-poo-poo." On the ground it drives its bill into the earth and produces a lower note, while in a tree it snaps its head with each note. It is no wonder that this unusual bird should have caught the attention of Bible writers for mention, even if only in a derogatory way.

IBIS, GLOSSY; *Plegadis falcinellus.* L 22″ W 37″

IBIS, SACRED (tinshemeth); *Threskiornis aethiopca.* L 30″ W 43″

The Hebrew word *tinshemeth* appears twice in the Bible (Leviticus 11:18 and Deuteronomy 14:16) where it speaks of birds that the Israelites should hold in abomination. The Authorized Version has translated the word as "swan," but it is almost surely incorrect, since swans are practically unknown in the Holy Land, and there would be no point to prohibit eating a bird that the people there did not know. The Septuagint translates it as *porphyrio,* or "ibis," and modern translators follow that lead or else are uncertain what to do with it. Both birds are possibilities, since they were common in the land of Israel. *Porphyrio* is the old name for moorhen, and comments on it appear under that heading.

The sacred ibis, now quite rare in Egypt, had a close association in the minds of the Egyptians with the rising and falling of the waters of the Nile, and for that reason it was revered. To them it was their god, Thoth, scribe to the other gods. No self-respecting nobleman would be buried without one of the birds embalmed at his side to record and embellish the events of his life. The Egyptian veneration of the bird may have been the reason why it was an abomination to the Israelites.

The ibis is a fairly tall white bird with black tail and wing primaries. The long, naked, black neck and head look as if covered with shoe leather. It is one of a number of species of ibises that include the white, the scarlet, and the glossy. The latter also frequents Palestine. They are closely related to the spoonbills.

41

Ibises are gregarious, usually nesting in large rookeries. When a flock travels they go in single file, alternately flapping and sailing in rhythm. When they fly by, the sailing motion begins at the head of the column and travels along in a wavy line to the rear.

JACKDAW; *Corvus monedula*. 13″—see Raven

Jackdaws, still smaller, also like to congregate in large numbers and usually make their nests in holes in buildings, often temples. They are black birds with gray napes and white around the eyes. Dr. Konrad Lorenz has recorded a number of interesting studies he made of the birds and their group behavior in his book *King Solomon's Ring*.

KESTREL—see Falcon

The kestrel is, however, common and stays the year round. It is similar in appearance and habits to the American kestrel, nests on cliffs and buildings, and lives by hunting small rodents, birds, and insects. In the grasshopper season it will live almost entirely on the insects. When a kestrel sees a movement in the grass it hovers a moment, then drops and seizes its prey in its yellow talons.

The lesser kestrel, also numerous, is a little smaller than the above, and the male lacks the spots on the back and wings. It is inclined to be gregarious, roosting in flocks in trees, and nesting in colonies on cliffs and in quarries.

Egyptian Kite

Black Kite

KITE, BLACK (ra'ah, da'ah, dayyah); *Milvus migrans*. L 21″ W 45″
KITE, EGYPTIAN; *Milvus aegyptianus*. L 21″ W 30″

Only Deuteronomy 14:13 uses the Hebrew *ra'ah*. The KJV translates it as "glede," an Old English term for the red kite, one of three Eurasian species sometimes called *buzzards* in England. The word *ra'ah* refers to sight or vision and would be descriptive of a number of birds in the eagle-hawk-vulture group. In the context it would most likely refer to the kite. Leviticus 11:14 refers to the same bird as da'ah and translators render it as "kite."

Kites were common in Bible lands, and they often gathered in flocks. The word *da'ah* sometimes gets translated as "vulture," when it should have been "kite," as in the following two texts: "There shall the vultures [kites] also be gathered, every one with her mate" (Isaiah 34:15); and "There is a path which no fowl knoweth, and which the vulture's [kite's] eye hath not seen" (Job 28:7).

Commonest and largest of the three species found in Palestine is the red kite. It feeds on small birds, mice, reptiles, and fish. Like the osprey, it can dive from great heights, catch a fish in its talons, and carry it off. The bird's wings are powerful, and the old name glede, comes from its habit of

43

KITE, RED; *Milvus milvus.* L 25″ W 60″

gliding on air currents. Because of its exceptional eyesight—as Job inferred—it does a lot of watching and seeing while soaring.

The black kite is another widely distributed species, abundant and easily seen. It is likely the one referred to in Isaiah, for it gathers in large numbers at the presence of carrion. Like gulls, these birds frequent the beaches, wharves, and town dumps for food.

The Egyptian kite is also quite dark in overall color. A sly thief, it will often raid poultry yards and also other birds of their food. Like the black kite, it prefers to stay around towns and villages and to feed on the garbage thrown there.

Kites typically have long, narrow wings and long, forked tails. The Old World species are in most cases larger and heavier birds than our slim American species. They appear to be more like the harriers except for the forked tails.

LAMMERGEIER—see Vulture, Bearded

LAPWING—see Hoopoe

MAGPIE—see Raven

JAY

Still another in our list of corvidae found in Palestine is the noisy, dashing magpie that flies around in its smart black and white plumage, flashing its long tail. Though not mentioned in the Scriptures, many of the Bible authors especially those who spent their lives in the wilderness areas, must have known it. Last of all, we will mention the jay in its white, black, and blue plumage. It is also common in Palestine, though not referred to in the Bible.

MARTIN, HOUSE

The house martin, still another swallow found in the Holy Land, also builds cup nests under the eaves. Blue-black above and white below, it much resembles the American tree swallow. In Europe the name *martin* applies to several swallows, while in America it refers only to the large, dark-bodied swallows that nest in high-rise apartment bird houses built especially for them.

MARTIN, SAND

The sand martin also dwells in Palestine. It is one of a group, like our bank and rough-wing swallows, that excavate tunnels in sandy banks and nest in them. The ancients would have included it in the term *swallow*.

MERLIN—see Falcon

MOORHEN; Gallinule (tinshemeth); *Gallinula chloropus*. L 13"

In Leviticus 11:18 and Deuteronomy 14:16 the KJV translates the word *tinshemeth* as "swan," a questionable choice, since swans do not live in the Holy Land. It is also thought to refer to the sacred ibis, as we have mentioned under that heading. Still another possible rendering is *porphyrio*, the old genus name for some of the gallinules.

The moorhen, or common gallinule, is likely the one meant, for it is widely known throughout the world as well as in Palestine. This rather dull-colored member of the tribe usually lives in marshes where leafy foliage such as water hyacinth or lily pads abound. The moorhen has rather long, thin toes, and it relies on them to support it on the floating vegetation. The bird's light weight, wide toe-spread, and constant activity

46

help to keep it above water. It is usually just stepping on to the next leaf as the one it previously stood on sinks under water. If it should fall in, no harm results, for it is a capable swimmer and diver.

The fowl has received its name because it is about the size of a hen, has a pointed bill, and unwebbed toes. However, it does not live on the moors and is not a hen, but more closely related to the coots and rail. With its red, pointed beak it catches frogs, insects, and small reptiles, but mostly it hacks at the seeds of aquatic plants. Usually it is busy trotting over mud flats or on lily pads, with its head and tail bobbing, or it may be swimming serenely in the open water. When startled on land, it will more likely run than fly.

NIGHTJAR; nighthawk (tachmas); *Caprimulgus europoeus*. L 10″
NIGHTJAR, EGYPTIAN; *Caprimulgus aegyptius*. L 10″

As with many other Palestinian birds, the nighthawk appears only in the two passages on dietary restrictions: in Leviticus 11:16 and Deuteronomy 14:15. Scholars have some doubt about whether *tachmas* should have been translated as nighthawk or whether the Bible writer intended the barn owl.

The nighthawk, or nightjar as it is known in England (probably because of its jarring call), does inhabit Palestine and thus warrants discussion here. It belongs to the goatsucker family; that includes also the frogmouths, potoos, and whippoorwills. Such birds all have large mouths that open from eye to eye. An old wives' tale that dates back to the time of

Aristotle held that they sucked the milk of goats at night.

The large mouth, lined with curved bristles on either side, equips the birds to fly through swarms of insects at night and gulp down hundreds of them. Researchers have found as many as 500 mosquitoes in the crop of one bird. Sometimes they catch large moths, and they have even been known to swallow small birds, probably by mistake.

The Egyptian nightjar is lighter in color than the European, and dwells in the southern deserts. It is probably similar to our whippoorwills, for it keeps up a persistent, loud, churring call, like that of the whippoorwill, rather than the familiar "beans" call of our careening nighthawk.

People see these birds less often than most, partly because they come out only on cloudy days or at night, but also because they rest on a branch lengthwise instead of crosswise as do most other birds. They lay their eggs in a slight hollow on the ground, where the mottled feathers of the bird provide camouflage.

OSPREY; fishing eagle (asniyah, ozniyah); *Pandion halietus.* L 22" W 60"

Though the Authorized Version mentions the osprey by name in Leviticus 11:13 and Deuteronomy 14:12, some other translations render *asniyah* as "black vulture." It is, however, quite plausible that the osprey is the bird intended since it is of worldwide distribution and a resident of the Holy Land.

This striking hawk, with snowy white underparts, black mask, and long, heavy legs, is not hard to identify. The bird appears frequently along the coast of Palestine and along its rivers but does not seem to be common around the Sea of Galilee, where one would expect it to be.

Living almost entirely on fish, the hawk is naturally an expert fisherman. It does not dive and catch fish in its beak as do the kingfishers, brown pelicans, or terns. Instead, it drops down with closed wings into the water and grabs the fish in its talons. Then it surfaces with a great splashing, and its long, powerful wings lift it up out of the water. Occasionally it grabs a fish that is too heavy for it to lift. One person observed a hawk that had to propel its fish to the shore to land it. Most of the fish it catches are surface feeders that anglers usually refer to as trash fish.

The horny talons of the osprey have barbed scales that help hold the fish after it is caught. If the bird grabs its prey tail first, it will turn the fish's head forward in the air before flying off with it.

Some eagles are also fond of fish but too lazy to search for their own. They wait till they see an osprey with its prey, then they threaten or strike the bird in flight, causing it to drop its meal. The eagle then dives under the osprey and often seizes the fish before it hits the ground.

Ospreys nest in tall trees and raise families of four or five. They teach them to fish, and when they succeed a great clamor of highpitched squealing and "peeping" that follows reminds one a bit of baby chicks.

OSSIFRAGE—see Vulture, Bearded

OSTRICH (ya'anah, bath ya'anah, renanah, chasidah); *Struthio camelus.* L 72"

We can have little doubt about the translation of *ya'anah* as "ostrich" in Job 39:13-18 of the Authorized Version of, but in other places the KJV translated bath ya'anah as "owl" when it also should have been "ostrich," as in the passages on diet restrictions in Leviticus 11 and Deuteronomy 14. Africans relish the bird.

A fine description of the ostrich appears in Job 39:13. However, in the first phrase, "Gavest thou the goodly wings unto the peacocks?" the use of "peacocks" is questionable. Their wings are unimpressive—the tail is quite another thing, however. It evidently should have referred to the ostrich, as it does in the rest of the text. The ostrich's "goodly wings" are the large, white plumes of the male, prized by the ancients. People in Bible times mounted the graceful plumes at the ends of rods, and the slaves of the wealthy used them to fan their masters in hot weather or to keep the flies off them. The plumes also served as crests on helmets or decorations on the bridles of chariot horses.

The book of Job pictures the ostrich as hardhearted and stupid: "Which leaveth her eggs in the earth, and warmeth them in dust, and forgetteth that the foot may crush them, or that the wild beast may break them. She is hardened against her young ones, as though they were not hers; her labor is in vain without fear; because God hath deprived her of wisdom, neither hath he imparted to her understanding" (verses 14-17).

Such was the general impression most desert dwellers had of the ostrich at that time, and it was regarded as accurate until more recent studies of the big birds have shown that things are not always as they seem. Ostriches mate for life, and the hen lays 10 to 12 eggs in a hollow she has scooped out of the sand. Sometimes other hens lay eggs in the same nest until it may contain as many as 30 or 40 of them. When the male—who helps care for the eggs—decides that there are enough, he will accept no more. The hens, unable to stop laying immediately, leave them in the sand near the nest. They are the ones that "the foot may crush" or "the wild beast may break."

The male incubates the eggs in the nest at night. On cool or cloudy days the better camouflaged female sits on the eggs during the day. On hot days, however, the bird buries the eggs in nearly a foot of sand that the sun keeps at an even temperature. One of the birds constantly watches the nest from a distance while feeding.

A note in a popular concordance explains that the reason the ostrich does not sit on the eggs is that her weight would crush them. This is not accurate, for the ostrich distributes its weight evenly over a large number of eggs as well as on her shanks, which fit between them. The eggs are hard-shelled and do not break easily. On ostrich farms the birds sit on the eggs without problems.

Prowling hyenas and jackals find the eggs lying around the nest, and they have difficulty biting through the hard and slippery shell. Vultures too are fond of the eggs, but fail to crack them with their beaks as well as to try to flying off with them, for they are too large and smooth to grasp. They have learned to pick up rocks, fly over the eggs, and "bomb" them.

The charge in Job that "she is hardened against her young ones, as though they were not hers" is true in the sense that the female does not show much concern about her young after they have hatched. The male is the one who looks after the brood, finds water for them, and shelters them under his wings at night. The precocious young are about a foot tall when hatched and gain about a foot a month at first, then they slow down a little. Eventually they reach six feet tall or more. They can run around within hours after hatching and find their food as can baby chicks. When threatened, they squat flat on the sand with their necks stretched out in front of them. Hunters seeing them with their heads hidden in grass thought they were burying them in the sand.

The statement that "God hath deprived her of wisdom, neither hath he imparted to her understanding" is apparently accurate, although, like most other creatures, ostriches are shrewd in areas that have to do with preserving their lives. Those who have raised ostriches admit that they are both ugly-tempered and stupid, and that they become more so with age. When we consider that they may live to be 100, we see that they have time to develop their negative traits.

"She scorneth the horse and his rider" (verse 18). The phrase calls attention to the fleetfootedness of the two-legged, two-toed bird. A man on horseback cannot hope to outrun an ostrich. To catch the birds, riders race them in relays. Ostriches tend to flee in large circles in order to stay in familiar territory, so the hunters cut off arcs of the circle in order to gain on them. In ancient times people sometimes caught the big birds in snares. They were not easy to trap because they are extremely watchful and have keen eyesight. Because the plumes were scarce, society reserved them for the wealthy.

The now extinct species of ostriches of northern Africa and Palestine were a little smaller than the ones currently living in southern Africa, but were formidable when cornered. Not only can the birds peck hard with their beaks, but they can kick forward and claw down with a powerful foot with enough strength to disembowel a man. Their real defense, however, is the speed with which they can cross the scrub-covered floor of the desert when pursued.

OWL, BARN; white owl (yanshuph); *Tyto alba.* L 14"

The Bible mentions several owls, and we will try, from the Hebrew terms and the context of the references, to identify at least some of them by their present names. The text names them variously yanshuph kos, lilith, and qippoz. Translators have rendered the terms as "great owl," "little owl," "screech owl," "long-eared owl," "short-eared owl," "white owl," "desert owl," "tawny owl," "fisher owl," "horned owl," "owl," and "ostrich." Also sometimes as "night creatures" or "night monsters." Ornithologists say that nine different species of owls presently live in the Holy Land, though some are quite rare. They believe that all those specifically mentioned in the Bible are still there. We will consider a number of the more common ones.

The barn owl has a worldwide distribution, and it also occurs in Palestine. One often sees it among ruins, abandoned buildings, and churches. Ordinarily it does not show itself in the daytime, but it has excellent night vision and finds its way around easily in pitch darkness. Its call is a screech, and this, with its pale body floating in the shadows, has given rise to many stories of haunting spirits. When Isaiah, in chapter 13, referred to the ruins of once-great cities, saying, "Owls shall dwell there,

OWL, EAGLE; great owl (yanshuph, qippoz); *Bubo bubo.* L 27"

and satyrs shall dance there" (verse 21), he may well have had the barn owl in mind.

The great owl, mentioned in Leviticus 11:17 and Deuteronomy 14:16 as an unclean bird, is most likely the tawny-colored eagle owl, a close relative of our great horned owl. The bird received its name of eagle owl because of its great size. It has a wingspread of nearly five feet. Like its American congener, it lives largely on big birds, which it catches asleep, and on rodents. The eagle owl is powerful enough to catch the large Syrian hares. The large owl's flight is strong and silent, and it will sometimes attack even humans by mistake.

On late winter nights the latter owls do a lot of serenading of each other with their ghostly "boo-hu," repeated several times. Their call may be what the prophet Zephaniah had in mind in chapter 2:14 when he said, "Their voice shall sing in the windows." The word translated "bittern" could more appropriately have been rendered "owl."

Isaiah 34:15 states, "There shall the great owl make her nest, and lay, and hatch, and gather under her shadow," referring again to the ruins of the great kingdoms of the prophet's day. The eagle owls do nest in just such places, also in the vacant nests of hawks and eagles, and in crevices of rocks where they have not only safety but also protection from the direct glare of the sun. They nest early in the season, often when snow still remains on the ground.

The KJV and other translations specifically mention the screech owl. The text in Isaiah quoted above in part, says, "The screech owl also shall rest there, and find for herself a place of rest" (verse 14). The barn owl was often called screech owl because of its call, but the smaller scops owl, also common in Palestine, is likely the one referred to here. It is a small owl with short ear tufts and comes in brown and gray color phases. Like our American screech owl, its call is not a screech at all but a long repeated tremelolike call, or a "piuww-uw-uw-uw."

The southern little owl is quite common in Palestine and is better known than most of the others, for it often ventures out in the daytime as well as at night. Appearing quite tame, it will perch on a post in the open and not move till one comes within a few feet of it. It lives largely on insects, small birds, rodents, and reptiles. A fast flier, it can even catch birds on the wing at times. The owl nests in tree cavities. However, it is not the European equivalent of our pygmy or elf owls, but belongs to a separate group of small, Old World owlets.

OWL, LITTLE (kos); *Athene noctua.* L 14"
OWL, LONG-EARED; *Asio otus.* L 14"

The tawny owl is quite common and has a wide distribution throughout Eurasia, including the Holy Land. Although about the size and color of the short-eared owl we often see flying low over marshes on cloudy days, it lacks the ear tufts on the forehead. The tawny owl and the barn owl are among the few that have black eyes. Like the barn owl and the little owl, it likes being around human habitations. Unlike the barn owl, however, it often appears during daylight hours.

The long-eared owl, though less common now, also lives in Palestine. A slim bird of the woods, it has long, upright ear tufts.

OWL, SCOPS; screech owl (lilith); *Otus scops.* L 8″
OWL, TAWNY; *Strix aluco.* L 15″

PARTRIDGE, CHUKAR; *Alectoris chukar.* L 13″
PARTRIDGE, DESERT (qore); *Perdix perdix hayi.* L 12″

The partridge, though several species inhabit Palestine, appears only twice by name in the Authorized Version of the Bible. In 1 Samuel 26:20 we find that David, who has spared Saul's life in the cave at Mount Hachilah during his flight from the first Israelite king, remonstrates with him, "The king of Israel is come out to seek a flea, as when one doth hunt a partridge in the mountains."

The desert partridge is a lighter-colored subspecies of the gray partridge that man has introduced into this country from Europe, and it is here generally referred to as the Hungarian partridge. These birds are fast runners and prefer to escape by running away between rocks and bushes, rather than by flying.

In Israel small boys armed with short sticks often chase them. They gang up on one partridge and pursue it, throwing their sticks at it above and below, to keep it from flying. In this way they hound the bird till it despairs of escape and gives up. That is the way David must have felt, as recorded in the first verse of the next chapter: "I shall now perish one day by the hand of Saul."

The Hebrew name *kore* means caller, and refers to the mating cries of the males in the desert mountains during the spring. Observers report that they are still common in the region of Adullam, where one can hear them calling to each other as they did in David's time.

The other reference (Jeremiah 17:11), "as a partridge sitteth on eggs, and hatcheth them not," is more accurately translated in the New International Version as "like a partridge that hatches eggs it did not lay." The passage calls attention to the fact that the birds lay a large number of eggs in a nest, as many as 20, and hatch them. The desert dwellers did not believe that one bird could produce that many, and reasoned that she probably stole eggs from other nests and brooded them as her own. This fact helps us understand the simile, which applies to a man who accumulates riches from others by unjust means—riches that will in the end desert him as the chicks do the hen.

The rock partridge and the similar chukar are also found in Palestine. Game hunters have introduced the chukar into the United States and the bird has adapted well to the dry western foothills. Still another partridge, a species of the francolins, lives in Palestine. It is larger than some we have just mentioned, but like them it prefers to run through the brush rather than fly. Its black-edged white feathers give it an overall gray appearance at a distance.

The terms partridge, grouse, and quail, as commonly used, are not

PARTRIDGE, FRANCOLIN; *Francolinus francolinus*. L 14"

58

definitive, but rather overlapping. Many call our ruffed grouse a partridge, and many of our small, western quails greatly resemble the true partridges of Eurasia. All are gallinaceous birds related both to the pheasants and to our chickens.

PARTRIDGE, GRAY
PARTRIDGE, ROCK; *Alectoris graeca.* L 13″

We might mention also two species of birds in Palestine that many often refer to as sand partridges. The NEB translates the term in Isaiah 34:15, which the Authorized Version renders as "great owl," as "sand-partridge." Both the black-bellied and the pin-tailed sandgrouse are common in Palestine. Such birds are really more closely related to the pigeons than to the partridges, but resemble the latter in size and habits. Sandgrouse (For illustration, see p. 67.) gather in large flocks, feed in sandy areas, and stay mostly on the ground. In the evenings they fly to water holes, where they wade in to their crops and take long draughts of water, drinking as pigeons do. They do not raise their heads between gulps to let the water flow down, as is the habit of other birds in drinking.

PEACOCK; PEAFOWL (tukkiy); *Pavo cristatus.* L 84″

The Hebrew word *tukkiyim* appears as "peacocks" in the KJV, but scholars have disputed that rendering. Some think it should have been guinea fowl that Solomon's navy brought back with them from Ophir with the alleged apes, as recorded in 1 Kings 10:22 and 2 Chronicles 9:21. Or it may have been just another kind of ape. On the other hand it is quite possible that Solomon's navy could have gone to India and have returned in three years, and if they did, they could easily have brought some of these plentiful, partly domesticated birds back with them to delight and astound their king.

The peacock, or male peafowl, is certainly one of nature's most strikingly beautiful birds, and it seems as if he knows it. He carries himself and his gorgeous tail with what appears to be unmitigated arrogance as he displays his plumage before anyone who will watch. He is able to spread the shimmering, ocellated plumes of his fanlike tail, shivering in a brilliant semicircle behind his cobalt blue body and crested head. Should danger threaten, however, he can quickly fold his fan and sneak away unnoticed into the jungle. Had Solomon been so fortunate as to have had some peacocks in his courtyard, I'm sure it would have delighted his beauty-loving soul.

In Job 39:13 we read, "Gavest thou the goodly wings unto the peacocks?" This too, it seems, is a mistranslation. It was really referring to the ostrich, as does the rest of the verse. Had it the peacock in mind, it would have mentioned the "goodly tail" rather than the wings, for the peacock's wings are quite ordinary.

PELICAN, DALMATIAN (qa'ath); *Pelecanus crispus.* L 65″ W 100″

The same KJV texts in Isaiah and Zephaniah that mention the cormorant and the bittern also speak of the pelican, and with no more justification than the other two. Leviticus 11:18 and Deuteronomy 14:17 proscribe it as unclean. Isaiah 34:11 and Zephaniah 2:14 refer to it as the personification of desolation. It also appears in Psalm 102:6, in which the writer bewails his miserable condition, "like a pelican in the wilderness." There is, again, uncertainty about the translation, but from the angle of natural history it could be correct. The pelican does usually nest on desolate, barren islands in lakes. Seeing a pelican at rest with its head laid back between its hunched shoulders, looking down the long bill resting on its crop, could well give the impression of miserable discouragement. No wonder the psalmist used such a picture to describe how he felt in affliction as he poured out his soul to God.

The Eurasian white pelican, found in the Holy Land, has a close relationship to the white pelican of the New World, and its lifestyle is quite similar. It is a large bird with hollow bones, a surprisingly light body that floats high in the water, and a large wingspread. Too clumsy to catch fish by diving in the ungainly fashion of the brown pelican or to swim after them under water like the cormorant, it has its own methods that seem to be quite effective. It scoops up surface fish while paddling. Sometimes, in formation with others of its kind, it drives schools of fish before it into shallow bays. The large bill and expandable pouch sweep back and forth under water, catching numerous small fish. Then it raises the bill, strains the water out, and swallows the fish. The bird does not use its gular pouch as a carrying bag to transport the fish to its young. Instead it stores them

PELICAN, WHITE; *Pelecanus onocrotalus.* L 65″ W 100″

in the crop, then at the nest regurgitates them into the pouch for the young to gobble up.

On land pelicans appear clumsy, but when they stretch their large wings and soar upward as a flock, circling to gain altitude, they are a sight to behold. The sunlight reflects from the white plumage above, while the undersides are in shadow, and the black primary wing feathers contrast sharply with the dazzling white of the rest of the bird. Pelicans are strong fliers and often fly long distances between their feeding waters and their nesting islands.

In addition to the white pelican, the Dalmatian pelican also inhabits Palestine. It is a light grayish bird, but has a closer relationship to the white pelican than it does the brown. The primary feathers in the wings are grayish underneath but black above. The pouch is bright orange in the mating season, as distinct from the yellow pouch of the white pelican. The Dalmatian pelican also has a yellowish wash over the breast. Both birds usually frequent freshwater lakes or brackish ponds rather than the ocean.

QUAIL (selaw); *Coturnix coturnix.* L 7"

The Old Testament refers to the quail three times. Exodus 16:13 records that shortly after the Israelites crossed the Red Sea, God sent them quail at evening, and manna in the morning. Numbers 11:31, 32 gives us the details of an extraordinary migration of quail that came in answer to the murmurings of the people for meat, and a plea of Moses for help from God. "And there went forth a wind from the Lord, and brought quails from the sea, and let them fall by the camp, as it were a day's journey on this side, and as it were a day's journey on the other side, round about the camp, and as it were two cubits high upon the face of the earth. And the people stood up all that day, and all that night, and all the next day, and they gathered the quails: he that gathered least gathered ten homers: and they spread them all abroad for themselves round about the camp." The third reference, in Psalm 105:40, alludes to this memorable event.

The European quail is a small, plump bird, smaller even than our bobwhite, though similar in shape and habits except for the fact that it is migratory. The birds seasonally gather in large flocks to migrate. In spring they come from Africa across Arabia to their nesting grounds over most of Europe, then in fall they return with their young ones. Since they are not strong fliers, they have to wait for a good tail wind to help them cross bodies of water such as the Red Sea or the Mediterranean. It explains how the "wind from the Lord" brought the quails from the Red Sea. They may have waited for some time and gathered in exceptionally large numbers to cover as great an area as they did. The way the account reads it might seem that the quails piled up nearly three feet deep over the whole camp and surrounding area. Actually the quails either ran or flew low, being near exhaustion, and the people with sticks were able to knock them down and harvest large numbers of the birds. From the record we find, too, that they dressed the ones they could not eat and spread them out to dry in the sun outside the camp. As it was, the people ate so many quail that they became sick, and many of them died.

Such quail migrations have happened quite often in the desert, but usually no one has been around to massacre them. In more recent times the Egyptians began to take advantage of them. They killed, dressed, and exported large numbers of the birds for table use. During 1920 their exports reached a peak of 3 million birds. As in the case of the passenger pigeon of North America, such slaughter could not last. Soon the big flocks vanished. With the introduction of better conservation measures, the quail are now coming back, but not in their former great numbers.

One way of catching quails that the Arabs used was to surround a flock and slowly drive them closer together to a central patch of low shrubbery. Then the men would wave their burnooses and concentrate the fleeing quail in the low bushes, throw their cloaks over them, take them out, and dispatch them.

Conservationists and game hunters have introduced European quail into the American southern states more than once in fairly large numbers. They seemed to do well till it was time to migrate; then they left and never came back. It is likely that they drowned in the Gulf of Mexico.

Ash-throated
Raven

Raven

RAVEN (oreb, choreb) (korax); *Corvus corax.* L 25″
RAVEN, ASH-THROATED; *Corvus umbrinus.* L 25″

Most Bible scholars usually consider the Hebrew word *oreb* to be broad enough to include various other members of the crow family, but in most of the uses in the Scriptures it does seem to refer to the raven. It is the first bird mentioned in the Bible. When the waters of the Flood began receding, Noah sent out a raven to test the earth's habitability (Genesis 8:7). But it did not return, indicating, carrion feeder that it is, that it was able to find plenty of food on the desolate land masses that now projected out of the water. Ravens still seem to find ample food on bleak northern seashores as well as on mountain crags.

The raven next appears in the parallel passages of Leviticus 11:15 and Deuteronomy 14:14 as unclean meat for the Hebrews. Then, in 1 Kings 17:4-6, we have the unique story of the ravens sent to feed the fugitive prophet, Elijah, on bread and meat while he camped at the brook Cherith during the famine that had come upon Israel.

Job 38:41, Psalm 147:9, and Luke 12:24 remind us of the Lord's care for the ravens, and in Isaiah 34:11 the raven's haunt signifies the desolation that would overwhelm some of the great kingdoms of the prophet's time.

The two-foot-long raven is the largest member of the crow family. The wedge-shaped tail and the fact that it soars much of the time are, however, more definitive in identifying it in flight. Its loud croak is quite distinct from the call of a crow, and a closer view shows a heavy bill and untidy feathers, especially on the throat. Usually ravens frequent the mountains, desert, or seacoast rather than urban areas, although a visitor to the Tower of London can see them walking around among the tourists. The raven, in common with most other members of the corvidae genus, is omnivorous in its feeding habits. Generally it nests in clefts among boulders in canyons, or on trees. There the mother broods her eggs while the father feeds her, and later also the young. Ravens are circumpolar in distribution and were quite common in Palestine during Bible times. In the Negev Desert the smaller ash-throated raven is still plentiful. Its light throat feathers are more obvious than are the hidden ones on the white-necked raven of the American southwestern states and Mexico.

Jackdaw

Rook

ROOK; *Corvus frugilegus.* L 18"

Rooks are also black like crows, slightly smaller, and distinguished from them by a white area around the base of the large bill. Their call is less harsh and more nasal than that of the crows. Gregarious birds, they not only nest in colonies but usually fly in groups. "And rooks in families homeward go, and so do I," as Thomas Hardy says in his poem "Weathers."

Because of their nesting habits we have given the name of rookery to any communal nesting area, even to places where herds of seals come to bear their young.

SANDGROUSE—see Partridge
SHAG—see Owl, Scops
SPARROW, DEAD SEA; *Passer moabiticus.* L 5 1/2"

SPARROW, HOUSE (sippor) (strouthion); *Paser domesticus biblicus.* L 5 3/4"

SPARROW, TREE; *Passer montanus.* L 5 1/2"

The scholars of the KJV generally translated the Hebrew word *sippor* and the Greek *strouthion* as "sparrow." In most cases the rendering should have been "bird," referring collectively to many of the small birds found in the countryside.

The birds Jesus refers to in Matthew 10:29-31, "Are not two sparrows sold for a farthing? and one of them shall not fall to the ground without your Father . . . Fear ye not therefore, ye are of more value than many sparrows," were not necessarily sparrows, though they could well have been included among them. Jesus just meant small birds that one caught in nets or snared.

In trapping the birds at night, one hung a light net on two poles next to a known roosting place of small gregarious birds, with a lighted lantern hung on the other side of it. Next one beat the trees with sticks or pelted them with rocks, causing the birds to fly toward the light and get entangled in the net. Then plucked, dressed, and skewered on sticks, they went to the marketplace. Most of them could have been sparrows, for they tended to roost in flocks, but they could also have been other birds with similar habits.

One reference in the Scriptures that more likely refers specifically to the sparrow occurs in Psalm 84:3: "Yea, the sparrow hath found an house, and the swallow a nest for herself, where she may lay her young, even thine altars, O Lord of hosts." Most of us who have had problems with house sparrows nesting in eaves or on air conditioners and in public buildings recognize this trait and can easily believe that the house sparrow would nest even on the altars of the Temple.

The sparrow the Bible writer most likely had in mind would be the ubiquitous house sparrow. A Shakespeare enthusiast who thought we should have all the birds in America mentioned in the famous bard's writings introduced it into the United States. The house sparrow and the European starling are two that many people believe we could well have done without.

The house sparrow is not related to other American sparrows, but is a weaver finch, a member of an Old World subfamily that includes some birds that build communal tent-sized, elaborately woven nests in trees in Africa. House sparrows themselves construct rather messy nests of twigs and feathers that are communal only to the extent that several pairs may nest in the same tree. Their musical repertoire consists mostly of harsh chirps rather than songs.

Such sparrows were more numerous in the United States and overseas during the horse and buggy days than they are now, because they made a good living off the grain that the horses wasted, and that which passed through undigested. They do not do as well in the automobile age, but they are smart enough to dodge cars skillfully. Since the passing of the horse they have learned to make good use of bird feeders and to survive hard winters through the bounty of bird lovers.

The tree sparrow of Europe, another weaver finch unrelated to our tree sparrow, was also common in the Holy Land, and merchants could well have sold it alongside the house sparrows at two for a farthing. Tree sparrows gathered in dense flocks during harvesttime and devoured much of the farmer's grain. He got even with them to some extent by netting some of them and selling them in the marketplace.

Tree sparrows appear similar to the male house sparrow, except that they have black spots on their white cheeks. Both sexes have similar markings.

The Dead Sea sparrow is another one common in that area. It builds nests of twigs in trees and bushes, and uses them year after year. In addition to the previous sparrows, there is the chaffinch, a more colorful bird in red, brown, blue, and gray, with white shoulder patches. It is abundant along the roadsides, especially in winter. The brightly colored goldfinch and the linnet also could have come under the name of *sippor* in the Bible.

SPECKLED BIRD (ayit sabua); see also Hyena (in volume 1, *Animals*)

The word *sabua* means "streaked" rather than "speckled" and the Septuagint translates it as "hyena." That fits the context of the passage better and is probably correct. We have dealt with it elsewhere under that heading.

STORK, BLACK; *Ciconia nigra*. L 38″ W 62″

The stork receives five mentions in Scripture. Two of the texts, Leviticus 11:19 and Deuteronomy 14:18, classify its flesh as unclean to the Jews. The reference in Jeremiah 8:7 calls attention to the regularity of the stork's migration flights, and the one in Psalm 104:17 alludes to its nesting habits. Zechariah 5:9 mentions the wings of a stork seen in a vision. There seems to be no doubt in this case that the KJV has correctly translated the Hebrew word *chasidah*.

The white stork does not nest in the Holy Land anymore, but it passes through in spring from its wintering grounds in Africa to its breeding area in Europe. One can often see it in flight, feeding on frogs, eels, reptiles, and mice in marshy areas or following the plowman in the fields, looking for insects in the freshly turned soil.

In Africa, when the height of the sun indicates that the winter is nearly over, the storks begin to soar in daily spiral flights, attracting others till a large flock has gathered. Then, with alternate soaring and flapping of their large wings, the birds, with necks and legs outstretched, travel north in loose, irregular flocks, sometimes at great heights, on their long flights to their breeding grounds.

Most gregarious birds, like geese and cranes, honk constantly as they

STORK, WHITE (chasidah); *Cinconia ciconia.* L 40″ W 66″

fly, to keep the flock together. Storks are mute. They lack the required muscles in their syrinx, or voice box. To compensate, they keep up a continual clatter with their beaks to enable straying members to hear where the main flock is and to head for it. The clatter also helps individuals to keep from colliding when the visibility is poor. Isaiah had evidently heard their noise for he says, "like a crane or a swallow, so did I chatter" (Isaiah 38:14). The crane and the stork look somewhat alike in flight, and the prophet could easily have confused the two. The contrasting black primaries in the white wings are also a good visual aid in keeping the flock together.

Storks usually fly only in the daytime and use major geographical features to orient themselves. In the central African flyway the Nile River with its tributaries guides them. Then they follow through Palestine, Asia

Minor, and Greece to Europe. A western race winters in central West Africa and follows the coast through the straits of Gibraltar to Spain. Some go by Sicily through Italy, and still another group comes from India through Asia Minor to Europe.

For centuries storks have received protection in most of Europe, and they find an enthusiastic welcome when they arrive. Householders mount cartwheels or large baskets above chimneys for them to nest on. It is regarded as a good omen for a house to have a stork family nesting on it.

When building the nest, the male brings the material, mostly sticks, and the female arranges it into a circular pattern with a slight depression in the middle, where she lays three or four eggs. The pair takes turns brooding, with the female generally on the night shift.

Storks mate for life and usually return to the same nests year after year. Their young find mates and also nest nearby.

In some villages nearly every house has a stork's nest on it. Since they are colony nesters, close proximity does not seem to bother them. Their feeding territory, however, has invisible boundaries, and each one patrols the family beat.

In towns the storks become almost as tame as pigeons. They walk about on the streets and in the marketplaces, picking up scraps of refuse, insects, reptiles, and vermin to feed their young. They act as the sanitary commission in villages that have none.

The white stork stands about three and a half feet tall, about as tall as our common egret. Its neck is short compared to the egret's, but its red legs are long and sturdy. The toes are short and slender, and the middle one does not have a comb as does that of the heron. The red beak is heavy, but sharply pointed.

When Jeremiah saw this large bird soaring overhead, striking in its black and white wing pattern, he felt impressed with its regular appearance every spring. One could depend upon it. "Yea, the stork in the heaven knoweth her appointed times; . . . but my people know not the judgment of the Lord," he lamented in chapter 8:7.

The psalmist, speaking of the stork, says, "the fir trees are her house." It does not seem to fit with what we have been saying about it nesting on rooftops, especially since the white stork does not even nest in Palestine. Here the reference is apparently to the black stork. Though similar in size and feeding habits to its white cousin, the latter nests in the tops of fir trees in the canyons of the Holy Land. It was common there, but more inclined to live away from towns and to feed in the marshes rather than in the streets. However, men sometimes tamed these storks, and they would follow their masters around as would a dog.

Barn Swallow

Red-rumped
Swallow

SWALLOW, BARN (deror); *Hirundo rustica.* L 7 1/2"

"And the swallow shall build a nest for herself, where she may lay her young, even thine altars" (Psalm 84:3).

Not many could identify 10 birds readily from the many that sing and fly about us daily. It is understandable, then why the naming of birds— the smaller ones especially—is often rather sketchy in the Scriptures, and why many get grouped under one designation.

The swallow, however, was distinct enough in the minds of several Biblical writers to deserve special mention. The species they had in mind was likely the common swallow that nests over most of the northern hemisphere and is known here as the barn swallow. It likes to build its mud cup nests under the eaves and roofs of houses, barns, and sheds. The birds bring the mud for their nests mouthful by mouthful and plaster it against the boards, strengthening it with straws and grass. In the cups they lay their eggs and rear their young. Sometimes the nests fall down and mess up the hay on the barn floor (or the altars in Bible times). The parent birds must start over again.

One reason why people notice and become acquainted with swallows is that they spend most of their time out in the open, hawking after flying insects, dipping over a pond to skim one off the surface or to gulp a drink. The Hebrew name *deror* means "freedom," and the graceful, seemingly effortless flight of these beautiful birds typifies it. The wise man (Proverbs 26:2) calls attention to the swallow's flight. Jeremiah refers to another aspect of the swallow's flight—its migration. "The crane and the swallow observe the time of their coming" (Jeremiah 8:7). The Palestinian swallows travel to still warmer lands for winter. In the fall they gather in large flocks, perform aerial maneuvers, then rest in long rows on wires till suddenly one day they all vanish.

Many people believed until recently that they dived into swamps and hibernated in the mud for winter. Now we know that they go to tropical lands, where they can find the insects on which they subsist. Their need for insect food governs their migratory timing. They have to feed as they go, and they do not come north any faster than the warmth of spring causes the flying insects to emerge. In spite of the legend of El Capistrano, they do not return on the same day every year. The time of their coming may vary as much as two weeks, but they do arrive when the time is right. That may be what Jeremiah meant when he said that they "observe the time of their coming."

Swallows twitter and squeak as they feed in the sky. Isaiah 38:14 mentions the trait: "Like a crane or a swallow, so did I chatter." As they fly through the air they will dive, like a nighthawk, through a swarm of insects with their mouths open from eye to eye, and gulp down dozens of them. Their beaks also, like those of the nighthawk, are armed with curved bristles at the sides to assist in capturing their prey.

SWALLOW, RED-RUMPED; *Hirundo daurica.* L 7"

Palestine has another swallow—the red-rumped—that builds mud nests. Its nest has a shape more like a bottle lying on its side, and the birds also stick it under the eaves or in the peak of the roof. The swallow enters and exits by the small neck opening. This bird is similar to our cliff swallow, both in its appearance and the shape of the nest, but its tail has a fork like that of the barn swallow.

BEE EATER; *Merops apiaster.* L 11"

The brilliantly colored bee eater, a graceful flyer, though unrelated to the swallows, lived in the Holy Land, and the Bible writers might have classed it with them. Its brilliant plumage could have dazzled the eye and excited the imagination of the Bible poets.

SWIFT, ALPINE; *Apus melba.* L 8"
SWIFT; *Apus apus.* L 6 1/2"
SWIFT, PALLID; *Apus pallida.* L 6 1/2"

No doubt other unrelated birds also fell into the swallow category. The swift, with its cigar-shaped body and bow-shaped wings, that spends all day in the air fluttering and soaring alternately as it chitters and squeaks while catching insects, must surely have impressed the ancients as being a swallow. It resembles them superficially, but ornithologists regard it as more closely related to the hummingbirds. These birds gather in large flocks before migration, swarm like mosquitoes in the air—then, toward evening, funnel down into the depths of some large chimney where they rest for the night. The European swift has a forked tail instead of one ending in bristles like the American one. Palestine also harbors the pallid swift, a lighter-colored desert bird; and the Alpine swift, a white-bodied bird with a dark band across its breast.

THRUSH, BLUE ROCK (sippor); *Monticola solitarius.* L 8″

In Psalm 102:7 we read, "I watch, and am as a sparrow alone upon the house top." The KJV has translated the Hebrew word *sippor* as "sparrow." Scholars now believe that the real meaning of the word is simply "bird," and most modern translations now read that way. The term includes most small birds that have not distinguished themselves enough by some outstanding characteristic to earn a separate designation.

The house sparrows in Palestine are the same species as we have in America, and as most of us will easily recognize, we can hardly consider them lonely birds. They are extremely gregarious so we seldom see one sitting alone on a housetop. The sparrow's song too is usually a noisy chatter rather than a lament. In the psalm quoted above, the author bemoans his lot and writes of how he cries as would a lonely bird.

In attempting to determine what species of bird the psalmist might have had in mind, scholars have concluded that it might be the blue rock thrush. This bird is a little smaller than, but quite similar to the English blackbird and the American robin. All three are thrushes and are fond of living in the vicinity of humans.

Anyone who has seen and heard a robin sitting alone in a tree in the yard singing his doleful "rain song" can understand how one could interpret the blue thrush's similar song as a lament. This thrush sometimes haunts lonely cliffs, ravines, and rocky hillsides, but is also common in towns and villages. The male sings a loud, plaintive, monotonous tune from the walls and rooftops of Jerusalem. The psalm, some scholars believe, originated during the Babylonian captivity and contains nostalgic expressions of things the captives remembered about their home country.

TURTLE DOVE—see Dove, Turtle

VULTURE, BEARDED; lammergeier (peres); *Gypaetus barbatus.* L 44" W 102"

VULTURE, BLACK (neshar, nesher) (aetos); *Aegyptus monachus* L 40" W 44"

VULTURE, EGYPTIAN; Gier Eagle; Pharaoh's Chicken (racham, rachamah); *Neophron percnopterus.* L 23" W 27"

The KJV also calls the Egyptian vulture the gier eagle in Leviticus 11:18 and Deuteronomy 14:17, where the Bible writer listed it with the unclean birds. The Hebrew word *racham* means love, and some have thought that the ancients gave it to the vultures because they do not usually clan together with the hordes of other vultures, but go around in pairs and appear to have a loving relationship, incongruous as it may seem to us among vultures.

The Egyptian vulture is about the size of our black vulture and has some of its characteristics even though it is not closely related. The young are a uniform dark brown with a gray neck till about their third year. Then they assume their breeding plumage which is a dirty white with dark-brown primary wing feathers; a bare, yellow face; and pink legs. They also have long, wedge-shaped tails.

These vultures are fairly tame, and again like our southern black vultures, they walk about the streets and farmyards looking for garbage or anything edible. Possibly for that reason they have received their other name, Pharaoh's chickens. Wildlife agencies protect them throughout most of their range in the warmer climates of southern Europe and Asia, and though never very numerous, they are reasonably common there. In spring one often sees them following the plow like gulls, picking up grubs and worms in the newly turned earth. They also kill many rats, mice, and lizards.

The Egyptian vulture has a fondness for nara melons which grow wild. The fruit contains a lot of water. The bird also likes ostrich eggs, but its bill is not strong enough to crack them open. They are also too heavy to lift, so the vulture picks up a rock and drops it on the egg. It will also take a rock in its beak, and with a sudden flick of the head, throw it at the egg to crack it—another example of a tool-using bird.

The bird nests on cliffs, but not in colonies, and does not seem to be concerned about whether its nest is accessible or not. Usually the female lays two eggs in a large, untidy pile of sticks that passes for a nest.

The Authorized Version translates the Hebrew *da'ah* or *da'ayyah* as "eagle," but judging by the context of several of the verses that use it, it is sometimes the griffon vulture that the writer has in mind. The latter vulture was plentiful in Palestine and often the birds collected in large numbers around dead animals. The verse in Matthew 24:28, "Wheresoever

VULTURE, GRIFFON (da'ah, da'ayyah); *Gypso fulvus.* L 42″ W 100″

the carcase is, there will the eagles be gathered together," suggests these large vultures rather than the more solitary eagle which is also less of a carrion feeder. Large flocks of griffon vultures assembled on battlefields.

Griffon vultures are considerably larger than the golden eagles, and their length and wingspread almost equals that of the lammergeier. They carry the bird swiftly, as indicated in the reference to it in 2 Samuel 1:23: "They [Saul and Jonathan] were swifter than eagles [vultures], they were stronger than lions." Lamentations 4:19 declares "Our persecutors are swifter than the eagles [vultures] of the heaven." One can distinguish the griffon vulture from the lammergeier when they fly. The former has broader, more rounded wings, a neck ruff, and a shorter, squared tail.

Vultures eyesight is exceptionally keen and they can spot a carcass a long way off. They cannot, however, see it for miles, as some claim from the fact that they gather from far away to a kill. When vultures soar they patrol a specific area of the sky, and they not only observe what is on the ground, but they also monitor other vultures within their visual range. When another descends to earth, the rest know that it has found food and they follow it. Still others more distant see them go and also head in that direction. Soon large numbers assemble at a newly discovered carcass.

The griffon vulture has a head and neck bare of feathers but sparsely covered with a coarse down. At the base of the neck is a white ruff into which the bird can pull the head and neck for warmth when resting or sleeping.

These vultures nest in rookeries on the high, inaccessible cliffs of canyon walls. Here each female lays a single egg, hatches it, and feeds the young. Like the young of most birds, they are even less attractive than their parents. The adults themselves look awkward and ugly when on the ground or perched sunning themselves, but once in the sky they sail majestically with grace and beauty.

The term *peres,* meaning "breaker," appears only in the parallel lists of unclean foods in Leviticus 11:13 and Deuteronomy 14:12. Here is one case in which scholars have agreed that the lammergeier is the intended one. The KJV reads "ossifrage," and other versions say "vulture," "tawny vulture," "bearded vulture," or "black vulture." The Latin *ossifragus* meaning "bone breaker," gives us a clue to the bird's activities.

When vultures gather in large numbers at a kill, they soon strip the carcass to a skeleton. The lammergeier then comes, picks off some of the smaller bones, and swallows them. Then it grasps the larger ones in its feet, rises on updrafts in the mountains, and drops the bones onto the bare rocks below, where they shatter to splinters. The bird then descends and swallows the fragments, which one of the most powerful digestion systems in the bird world soon takes care of. The lammergeier can lift and crack even the leg bones of a horse or cow. It will also seize tortoises and smash them on the rocks to get through the shells.

With one of the longest wingspreads of any bird in the Old World, the lammergeier's long, pointed wings and wedge-shaped tail carry it to heights of 25,000 feet in mountain updrafts. That is nearly as high as Mount Everest's 29,000 feet and higher than any other bird has been known to fly.

The name lammergeier means "lamb vulture." Folklore accuses it of carrying off lambs, goats, and even babies, but the charges remain largely unproved. It has the short-clawed feet of a vulture, and they are not suited to killing and grasping as are those of eagles. It does, however, when it sees an ibex, wild goat, or even a hunched-over hunter at the edge of a cliff, sometimes swoop down and attempt to knock them over with its wings, to feed later from the carcass that has smashed on the rocks below. In practice, it lives almost entirely on bones and carrion.

The enormous nests of the lammergeiers perch high on inaccessible cliffs, and the birds add to them year after year until they may consist of as much as a wagonload of sticks, sod, and moss heaped up in a rough pile. Here the female lays one egg, hatches it, and feeds the young. As with most other large birds, the young take more than a year to mature. Because the immature birds are black, people sometimes call them black vultures, but that is still another species also found in Palestine. As the young grow they acquire the black mask, red eye, and bristly, black beard from which the lammergeier has gotten its other name of bearded vulture. The back is grayish black, and the underparts, including the feathered legs, are a light buffy orange in color.

OTHER
BIBLE CREATURES

Amphibians

FROG, GREEN (sephardea) (batrachos); *Rana esculanta.* L 3"

The only mention of frogs in the Old Testament occurs in the record of the second Egyptian plague in Exodus 8:1-15, and in the two texts in Psalms that refer back to that event. In the first of the plagues Moses stretched his rod over the River Nile, causing the waters to turn to blood and all the fish to die. The amphibious frogs in the river, however, did not die. But in the second plague God caused them to leave the polluted water and to scatter all over the land, into houses, beds, and even the kneading troughs of the Egyptian housewives. Here they died, and the people gathered them together into stinking piles to rot and to be eaten by vultures.

Such a plague today probably would not affect us in the same way as it did the Egyptians, since our houses are more or less frog-proof; but it could tie up traffic on our highways. In the Egyptian's somewhat doorless dwellings it was quite a calamity. The Egyptians worshiped a half frog-half woman goddess named Heqet. She was a patroness of birth and a symbol of the beginning of things. Egyptian art pictures her as having a frog's head and a woman's body. God also evidently intended the plague to discredit her.

Watered as it is by the Nile and its many channels in the marshy delta, Egypt was the home of millions of frogs. Their numbers did not constitute the plague so much as the fact that they left the river and marshes and invaded the houses.

The most common frog in Egypt is the green frog. It is quite similar to the green frog found in American and European streams and marshes. A medium-sized frog, about three inches long, it is quite a bit larger than the small spring peepers and other tree frogs, but it is only about half the size of the large bullfrog. The green frog lays its eggs in the marshes in spring. There they hatch into tadpoles and evolve into air-breathing adults. They spend nearly all their lives in and around water, and their survival depends on keeping their skins damp. Perhaps that is the reason that the frogs of the plague died when they left the water and entered the houses.

In the New Testament Revelation 16:13 mentions the frog: "I saw three unclean spirits like frogs come out of the mouth of the dragon, and out of the mouth of the beast, and out of the mouth of the false prophet." Here the Bible writer apparently uses them as a symbol of loathing or repulsiveness.

Fish

FISH (sha'ar dag dagah) (ichthus)

Even though the Jewish people had no direct access to the sea most of the time that they lived in Palestine and they had few lakes and rivers, fish were still important in their diet, and Scripture refers to them quite often. In the land of Egypt, of course, they caught fish in the Nile. Later, when they wandered in the arid wilderness, they thought back fondly to that time. "We remember the fish, which we did eat in Egypt freely" (Numbers 11:5).

BARBEL, LONG-HEADED; *Barbus barbus flaviatalis.* L 20"

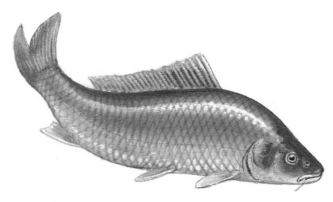

CARP; *Carpinus carpio.* L 36"

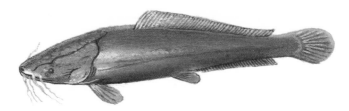

CATFISH; *Clarias lazera.* L 30"

DORADO; *Coryphaena hippurus.* L 60"

We cannot be sure how near they came to the waters of the Red Sea or the Gulf of Aqaba during their wilderness period, but it is likely that they became acquainted with some of the fish in them. During Solomon's time his ships may have sailed to the Indian Ocean, and we know that Hiram's Phoenician fleet fished in the Mediterranean and elsewhere. Nehemiah 13:16 tells us that the Phoenicians sold fish at the Fish Gate, located in the middle of the north wall of Jerusalem. Merchants also brought fish from the Sea of Galilee to the fish market there.

The Sea of Galilee and Lake Hula upstream from it (formerly known as The Waters of Merom) contains large numbers of freshwater fish, and so

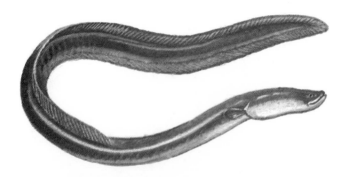

EEL, EUROPEAN; *Anguilla anguilla.* L 60"

EEL, MORAY; *Gymnothorax eurostus.* L 60"

does the Jordan River. Also most Palestinian streams contain fish, at least during the rainy season when they have water running in them. The Dead Sea, however, has too strong a mineral content for fish to tolerate.

To the north of Israel, along the coast, with their chief cities of Tyre and Sidon, lived the Phoenicians. A seafaring people, they not only traded with other nations, but also went to sea for sperm and other whales early in Biblical history. They were also active fishermen and, as we have seen, sold fish to the Hebrews.

Among the biblical references to fish are Leviticus 11:10-12 and Deuteronomy 14:9, 10. They distinguish between the clean and unclean fish. Those with fins and scales were clean, while those without were unfit for food to the Israelites. Considerable discussion has arisen since then on just which ones the taboo included and which ones it did not. In general, of the fish that the Jews were likely to catch, the most common unclean ones were the catfish and the eels, though a number of others can also fall in that category.

The most important of the unclean fish are the giant catfish. They

MULLET; *Mugil cephalus.* L 27"

REMORA; Sharksucker; *Echeneidae naucrates.* L 24"
SOLE; *Solea solea.* L 8"
STARGAZER; *Uranoscopus scaber.* L 13"
STURGEON; *Acipenser oxyrhynchus.* L 80"

reach more than two feet in length, often considerably longer, and used to be quite common in the Sea of Galilee and the Jordan River. On their lips grow several long, fleshy barbels that are apparently sense organs to help them find worms and underwater insect life as they root around in the muddy banks of the river or lake. Their flesh is said to be disagreeable in flavor, and it is hard to digest because it is so oily and gelatinous. Their swim bladders used to serve as the raw material for a coarse isinglass. People employed this forerunner of plastic to preserve eggs and other food items. Most fish are silent, but when caught the catfish will squeak like a kitten.

American eels have fine scales, but the European ones found in Palestine are scaleless. Lamprey eels and hagfish also live in Israel's waters. They, too, are scaleless, and, though forbidden to the Jews, are considered rather tasty. The European eels and the American ones both spend most of their lives in fresh water streams, but go to deposit their eggs in separate spawning grounds in the Sargasso Sea, east of Bermuda. There they die, and the young, transparent elvers find their way back the next spring to

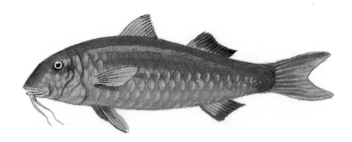

SURMULLET; *Mullus barbatus.* L 15"

their ancestral streams. The males stay in tidal waters, but the females go far upstream.

The large moray eels grow from four to six feet long and frequent Mediterranean waters. The Jews considered them scaleless, but they have fine scales underneath their slimy exterior. The Romans prized the fish, keeping them alive in pools, ready for a feast.

Sturgeons have five rows of bony plates over their bodies instead of scales. They live in the ocean or in large inland seas and come up the larger rivers to spawn in the spring. Although they can grow up to 18 feet long, usually they reach less than half that. People best remember them for the large number of eggs they bear, known to food connoisseurs as sturgeon roe, or caviar. Other fish in the unclean category that the Jews might have come in contact with were sharks, which have barbed shields instead of scales; the boxfish, which has a body covered with fused hexagonal plates; and rays, which are smooth skinned. All of them are saltwater fish.

Among clean fish the ones most widely caught and eaten in the Holy Land would have been the carp. Like the catfish, it also has a few barbels on its lips. Furthermore, it too digs in the mud for aquatic animal and plant life. Such grubbing often destroys the eggs and habitat of more desirable fish, and for that reason sport fishermen do not like the carp. It does not take a fly-baited hook, but one can sometimes catch it with bread or macaroni. The fish has large scales and is related to the goldfish, chub, dace, and many other minnows, but grows to a much greater size than they do. The carp has now spread over much of the northern hemisphere.

The long-headed barbel, also related to the carp, was a plentiful species in the Sea of Galilee, one that fishermen could easily catch in nets or even sacks as it rooted in the shallow water. Probably one of the principal fish taken by the fishermen disciples of Jesus, it might have been the one Christ broiled for them on the shore of Galilee after His resurrection. The barbel

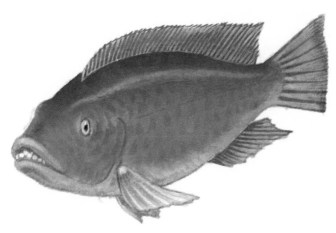

TILAPIA; *Tilapea galiea.* L 15"
TUNA; *Thunnus thynnus*

is a tough fish that can live in waters where other fish die. The Jews kept them fresh in garden pools, to use as needed. It seems too that they raised them in pools. The Song of Songs mentions the "fishpools in Heshbon" (7:4). In Isaiah 19:10 we find that the Egyptians also made sluices and ponds for fish. Most likely they contained carp, barbels, and other related fish. The Israelites today breed fish in extensive artificial ponds.

The tilapia of Galilee was another common edible fish. Some call it St. Peter's fish because tradition has it that Peter was eating one when he first heard of Christ's resurrection. The fish belongs to the family Chichlidae, one in which the adult males care for the eggs and young by holding them in their mouths till they can look after themselves. The fathers sometimes appear to be chewing them, but that is just part of the cleaning process. If the hatched young keep coming back after they can take care of themselves, the father may indeed eat them. Fast breeders, they will thrive in ponds.

The Nile perch was abundant in Egypt, and related species frequent most European streams. It is similar to the American yellow perch, brown above and silvery white below, with dark crossbands on the body, bright vermilion on the lower fins and sharp spines on the dorsal one.

Among the saltwater fishes the mullets have a wide distribution, and they thrive in the warm, shallow seas around Palestine. Fishermen call them "jumpers" because they often leap out of the water in unison. One can fry them in their own fat. Mullets get caught in nets not only in the ocean but also in streams that they occasionally ascend.

The golden-orange surmullet, also called the red mullet, is not a true mullet, but it is another good eating fish that the people of Bible lands prized. Israelites sometimes raised them in garden pools, and some of the Romans took better care of them than they did of their slaves. Their brilliant colors change as they die.

The tuna inhabits both the Mediterranean and the Red Sea, and the Phoenicians caught and sold it. It can weigh up to 300 pounds and has a good-tasting flesh. The bonito, a smaller relative, also comprised part of the fisherman's catch.

The large, brilliantly colored dorado of Mediterranean waters provided another significant part of the diet. The Romans kept them alive in pools before a feast. They entertained their guests by allowing them to watch as they killed the fish, so they could see the evanescent colors change as it expired. Then they roasted the flesh over fires and fed it to the people. In this way the guests could be sure they were eating fresh fish—if they still had the stomach to do so after watching it die.

On the shallow bottoms of both the Mediterranean and Red seas lives the stargazer which ancient fishermen brought up in dragnets. Extremely ugly, the fish seems to combine head and body in one. It lies half buried in the mud, dangling a small, red filament on a spine above its nose. When it has attracted a fish to it, the stargazer suddenly opens its cavernous mouth and gobbles it up.

The Jews refer to the sole, one of the best eating of the flatfish, as "Moses Our Teacher." Legend has it that when the Lord parted the waters of the Red Sea at the command of Moses, He parted the sole also. The halves later rejoined, but they can be easily separated again. This flatfish lies on the bottom of the sea, with both eyes on the upper side, and lives on crustaceans.

A curious verse in Ezekiel 29:3, 4 perhaps alludes to the remora, or sharksucker. God tells the prophet to prophecy against Pharaoh, king of Egypt, whom He compares to a dragon, or, in chapter 32:2 to a whale (sea monster) who claims the seas and rivers for himself. Ezekiel says, "I will cause the fish of thy rivers to stick unto thy scales, . . . all the fish of thy rivers shall stick unto thy scales." The remora, though it can swim quite well on its own, attaches itself by means of a suction device on the top of its head to larger fish such as sharks and porpoises and travels with them. It does not suck their blood like the lamprey, but is just a hitchhiker, feeding on the leftovers of their meals. The text may refer also to the freshwater lampreys and hagfish, since the passage mentions rivers.

Fishing

The Israelites had several methods of catching fish. Some they obtained by means of hooks (chakkah) (agkistron) attached to their lines. Christ told Peter to "cast an hook, and take up the fish that first cometh up" (Matthew 17:27), and in it he found the coin with which to pay Caesar's tax. They did not have sophisticated fishing poles, reels, and flies, as we do now, but they ingeniously made their hooks from bone, thorns, or metal. Fastening them to linen lines, they baited them with worms, minnows, or locusts. A stone attached to the end of the line kept it underwater, and a leader with a hook on it dangled about a foot or two back of the rock. The fisherman then held one end of the line, which lay coiled at his feet, with one hand, and with the other he twirled the weighted end and threw it as far as he could into the water. Then he drew it back slowly with jerky movements to make the bait seem alive. When a fish struck, he unceremoniously dragged it ashore.

If a fisherman had several lines to throw in, he would fasten the ends of the lines to willow stakes pushed into the damp mud of the river bank. The current would float the leaders downstream to tempt the fish, and the rock anchors would hold the ends in place. Then the fisherman could sit in the shade of a tree and watch for the telltale jerking of a peg to let him know when he had hooked a fish. Or if he had other things to do, he could compress balls of silty mud and place one on the top of each peg. Then he could come back some time later and pull in the lines on the pegs that had the mud balls knocked off.

For fish in the lakes or seas the fishermen trolled lines behind their boats and hauled their catches in. We have records of Phoenician sailors harpooning and bringing in to shore large whales at least 2,000 years before Christ. Without doubt, they also hooked and brought in tuna and other large fish in the same way quite early in biblical history.

The Bible often mentions nets (diktuon), and fishermen of that time used several kinds of them. One was a circular throwing net (cherem) (amphiblestron). Small stones weighted down its circumference, and the fisherman, standing on the shore or in the shallow water, tossed it out with a dexterous, centrifugal flip that spread it out open as it settled in the water, trapping fish under it. Then the fisherman drew on his line, and a sphincteral movement drew the edges of the net together. Holding the fish in the net bag, he then hauled them ashore. People still use this type of net in many tropical countries today, and it is as effective as ever at catching shallow-water fish.

The fishermen hauled dragnets (mikmoreth) (sagene) along the bottom of the shallower ocean shelves or lakeshores to bring to land some of the mud-loving fish and crustaceans found there. A gill net in streams would catch spawning fish as they migrated. Seine nets, with floats on the upper edge and weights on the lower, surrounded and trapped fish in the lakes. One could either pull them to shore or haul them into the boats. Sometimes more than one crew would join their nets together and divide the catch among themselves.

It is understandable that such a net would entrap many different kinds and sizes of fish. The parable Jesus told in Matthew 13:47, 48 probably referred to a seine net. He said that the fishermen "drew [it] to shore, . . . and gathered the good into vessels, but cast the bad away." They threw away not only the unsalable trash fish but also those classed as unclean. The net probably contained no extremely small fish, for they would have slipped through its meshes. The slippery eels probably did the same.

The story regarding nets that first comes to mind is likely the one in which the disciples had fished all night, caught nothing, and were coming in to land when they saw Jesus standing on the shore. He told them to "launch out into the deep" (in the Luke 5:4 version). They felt that it was useless to do so, but at His word they went out. The result is that they encountered a school of fish so great that the net threatened to break. With the help of their partners they managed to bring it to land.

Most fish in Galilee spend the daylight hours in the moderately shallow waters near the mouth of the Jordan, not far from Bethsaida, or at Seven Springs, near Capernaum. Here fishermen catch them with seines or dragnets. At night the fish stay in the deep water under the steep eastern shore, or where the mineral springs well up. Peter and his friends knew this and were certain that fishing in the deep water after daybreak was of no use. For that reason they regarded the great haul as a miracle and not just a coincidence.

The Gospels contain two similar miracle stories, one of the feeding of the 5,000 on five loaves and two small fishes (Mark 6:30-44), and another time 4,000 on seven small loaves and a few fishes (Mark 8:1-9). The loaves were probably small barley cakes, and the fish were evidently minnows, probably dried. The people often ate bread with small fish on it instead of butter, or they made the fish into a paste or dressing. Barley loaves probably needed something to make them palatable.

Broiling was another common way of preparing fish in Bible times. When Jesus appeared to His disciples in the upper room after His resurrection they believed that He was a ghost or spirit. To show them that he was flesh and blood, He asked for something to eat, and they gave Him some broiled fish and a honeycomb (Luke 24:42). Later, on the shore of Galilee, He broiled some fish over a fire, and when His disciples came to land, they ate the fish and some bread together. Christ must have broiled the fish by roasting it over a fire on the shore of the sea (John 21:9-13).

Insects

ANT, HARVESTER (nemalah); *Messor semirufus.* L 1/4"

Only Proverbs 6:6-8 and 30:25 mention the ant, but both are honorable mentions, and interesting. Solomon, in giving counsel to young men, said, "Go to the ant, thou sluggard; consider her ways, and be wise; which having no guide, overseer, or ruler, provideth her meat in the summer, and gathereth her food in the harvest"; and Agur, son of Jakeh, says, "The ants are a people not strong, yet they prepare their meat in the summer."

The biblical statements puzzled entomologists for some time. They knew of the foraging habits of ants, of their complex colonies, and of their apparent industry and wisdom; but where had Solomon seen them gathering food during harvest and storing it for a time of need? Then in 1871 a British naturalist discovered the harvester ants living in several Mediterranean countries and other dry areas around the world.

Harvester ants live in colonies underground that open at a central entrance elevated by a cone of earth excavated from below. The cone helps shed water during a rainstorm. To further facilitate the runoff of water, the ants clear all obstructions, grass, pebbles, weeds, and trash away to make a smooth area four to six feet in diameter around the entrance.

My introduction to an American species of harvester ants came in Wyoming. When taking off from an airport in a small plane, I saw the grassy hills all pockmarked with small circles of bare ground spaced out evenly in the dry grass. At that time I had no idea what could have caused such an unusual geometric pattern. Later, when driving through a similar area in Colorado, I saw close at hand that it was the work of harvester ants.

They pile all the cuttings from their clearing at the circumference of their circle as mulch, then gather grass seeds from the surrounding area to store in their underground chambers. They sort and hull the seeds in one of the first rooms. The hulls they remove and leave at the perimeter, and the good seeds they carry to lower chambers. Some worker ants are extra large and have exceptionally heavy jaws. Chewing the seeds into partially masticated "ant bread," they feed it to the young and other workers. Harvester ants favor a certain species of small, white, flinty seeds that, under the microscope look like rice. Some have called the seeds "ant rice."

If during a prolonged rainy spell the stored seeds should get wet, the ants take them out and dry them on the first sunny day. The good ones go back when dry, but should some have already sprouted, they get dumped in the rubbish at the outer margin of the yard. The sprouted seeds usually grow and soon form a luxurious stand of the ants' favorite crop right around their farmstead. The ants carefully snip off and weed out any undesirable plants from their garden. When the ant rice ripens, they harvest the seeds.

The practice has given rise to the idea that the ants intentionally plant their rice. Actually it may be just incidental through the discarding of seeds that would otherwise rot. Surely Solomon, in observing these methodical insects, had reason to think the ant wise. Harvester ants usually live in areas where growth is seasonal, and one way they can continue to exist is to gather food when it is abundant and to store it.

Solomon makes another interesting observation. He notes that the ants do all their work and run their complex organization without having a "guide, overseer, or ruler." Every ant colony has at least one queen, and the life of the community centers around her, but she is no leader or ruler. She is just an egg-laying machine. An ant colony has no dictator or general manager to direct itself, to see that the necessary work gets done, and that everyone does his fair share. How does it all operate? What are the incentives? Observant scientists have found some of the answers.

Worker ants survive as long as seven years, worker bees only a few months. That means that any colony of ants will have quite a number of workers who have lived through several seasons, and who know what to do and how. Still, they apparently do not act as straw bosses, telling others what to do while they watch. Instead, they are the initiators. They know where to find food and what to do with it, and so they begin the action. Others see them doing something and follow their example.

Entomologists have found ants more adept than most insects at solving mazes. The tiny creatures seem to show quite a bit of originality also in finding ways of circumventing barriers we contrive to keep them out of places where we don't want them. However, when locked in some instinctive drive, they can also be quite stupid. Ants started around the rim of a bowl just kept following each other around until they died one by one. Sometimes they seem to justify Mark Twain's contention that they are the most stupid of insects, especially when they pull in several different directions on some food. Ants can show quite a lot of individual differences, even though to us they may all appear to be clones.

People thought at one time that ants posted sentries at some distance from their hills to warn them of approaching danger. Closer observation leans to the opinion that these are not sentries, for they are in a position of rest with their legs under them and their feelers down.

Ants, in all their varied genera, have gone into many other occupations than harvesting. Army ants march through the jungle in large bands, eating everything edible in their path, and taking their queen and young with them. Carpenter ants hollow out dead trees with tunnels as termites do. Dairying ants tend to aphids and milk them for the sweet juice they draw out of plants. Leaf cutters grow mushrooms underground on beds of compost made from green leaf pieces they have gathered. And honey ants keep certain of their workers with greatly distended abdomens to store honey until needed. Some ants are thieves and panhandlers, living off other ants. Other kinds rob colonies of their pupae to raise as their own slaves. One cannot help being impressed when studying ants, as Solomon was.

BEE, BANDED (deborah); *Apis fasciata.* L 5/8"
  HONEY (debash) (meli).
  HONEYCOMB (ya'ar).

The Bible several times describes the land of Canaan as "a land flowing with milk and honey" (Exodus 3:8). Ancient documents found in Egypt use a similar description. However, even though bees do live there, scholars believe that the term probably refers to a sugar syrup concentrated from grape juice. The native bees build their hives in tree cavities and cracks in rocks, and gather nectar from the many flowers and flowering trees that abound even in the desert.

During the time of Saul his soldiers passed through a woods where wild honey dripped from the trees. They were starving, yet they couldn't touch it, for their king had commanded that no man should eat until they had defeated the enemy. His son, Jonathan, who had not heard the edict, poked his spear into a comb and ate the honey (1 Samuel 14:24-30).

Deuteronomy 1:4 refers to the combative nature of bees: "The Amorites . . . chased you, as bees do." Psalm 118:12 declares, "They compassed me about like bees." Travelers report that bees infest some of the narrow canyons in the Holy Land.

The important thing about bees, however, is that they produce honey, and so it was in Bible times. In Deuteronomy 32:13, in speaking of how God would care for His people, Moses says, "He made him to suck honey out of the rock." Genesis 43:11 tells how Jacob instructed his sons to take a gift of "a little honey" for the prime minister of Egypt. Again some commentators believe that he meant, not bee honey, but concentrated grape or other fruit syrup, since there would be plenty of honey in Egypt. But one could also use that argument against the spices and nuts.

Judges 14:8, 9 recounts the story of Samson finding a swarm of bees in the carcass of the lion he had killed on his previous trip to Timnath, and of how he ate and shared the honey with his parents without telling them where it came from.

In Isaiah 7:18, in connection with a prophecy that the Messiah should be a Nazarite and eat butter and honey (verse 15), we read that "the Lord shall hiss . . . for the bee that is in the land of Assyria." The hissing is more in the nature of "psst," a common way of catching someone's attention without alerting everyone. The Arabs also called bees this way to get their attention.

Man domesticated bees early in his history, and the methods of bee culture in some Bible lands probably changed little until recently. Beekeepers stacked earthen vessels on their sides and partly covered them with earth to keep them from becoming too hot from the sun. Then they introduced swarms into their ready-made hives. Getting the honey from them was the hard part.

Some more progressive householders built the cylindrical pots into the walls of their houses with the open end out and the bottom end exposed inside the house. The swarm then worked to fill the pot with honey. When the family wanted some, they would gently tap on the inside of the pot till the bees, annoyed by the noise, flew out. Then by means of a cord they dropped a trapdoor from inside to close the bees out of the hive. Removing the bottom of the pot, they could spoon the honey out. Leaving the eggs and larvae inside, they put the bottom back so the bees could make more honey.

The Israelites regularly ate honey when they had it, often with bread. Sometimes they would consume it in the comb (Luke 24:42), and at other times they let it drip out and purified it. John the Baptist ate it with his locusts, and it no doubt helped to supply elements that his sparse diet might lack.

Israelites today raise hybrid American and Italian bees in modern hives and remove the honey with electric extractors not far from some bee farmers who still use some of the primitive methods described above.

BEETLE—see Locust

BORER, VINE—see Weevil

CANKERWORM—see Locust

CATERPILLAR—see Locust

CRICKET—see Locust

CRIMSON WORM (tobath shani) (kokkos); *Kermes ilicis.* L 1/4"

   SCARLET (tolath shani) (kokkinos).

Crimson was one of the three sacred colors (with purple and blue) used in the furnishing of the tabernacle and Solomon's Temple. In 2 Chronicles 2:7, 14; and 3:14 we read of the craftsmen who could produce and work with the various materials, including crimson. Isaiah 1:18 gives us the comforting message, "Though your sins be as scarlet, they shall be as white as snow; though they be red like crimson, they shall be as wool." The book of Jeremiah speaks of being clothed in crimson. It was a highly prized dye employed in coloring the finest linens and silks for the hangings of the Temple and also for the garments of the rich.

Crimson dye came from the crimson worm, also known by its Arabic name, kermes, an insect found on the scrubby oaks that grow on the hills of Palestine and other Mediterranean countries. It is one of the scale insects that orchardists have trouble with. The female is about one quarter of an inch long, has a shiny, red-brown, convex shell. Fastening itself on oak twigs, it appears like a gall. The much smaller male spins a cocoon and secures himself to the undersides of leaves. The shell of the female soon fills with numerous, oval, bright red eggs that hatch into larva while still inside. They are the crimson worms.

The crimson worker (he probably becomes more or less crimson at the job) collects the females by scraping them off the twigs onto a sheet spread below. Then he carefully dries and compacts them into egg-sized balls for the market. The dyer soaks the balls in water, and the color bleeds out, making the water deep red. After he has strained the shells and other insoluble matter out of the liquid, he will dye the thread or cloth.

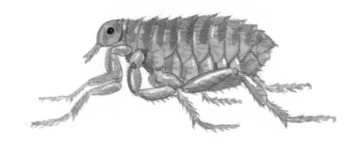

FLEA, HUMAN (par'osh); *Pulex irritans.* L 1/30"

This minute insect is, or at least has been, exceptionally prevalent throughout the Middle East and most tropical countries. Only 1 Samuel 24:14 and 26:20, where David remonstrates with Saul—"After whom is the King of Israel come out? after whom dost thou pursue? after a dead dog, after a flea"—does the Bible mention the creature. David did not have to explain further. All, from the beggar to the king, knew from personal experience what fleas were—how small and insignificant they were, yet how irritating. There were so many of them that one just took them for granted and hardly felt them anymore. Natives of flea infested countries find it amusing that the insects should bother a visitor. Mr. David Urquhart, an experienced traveler in the Middle East in the 1800s, thought that fleas might serve as a wholesome skin irritant for the natives, and that about two mouthfuls of every meal went to feed the pests.

Most of us know something about fleas from having dogs or cats as pets, and from struggling to control their fleas during hot weather. We may have even experienced their bites and seen them as they hopped erratically away. They are barely visible insects with six comparatively husky legs attached to a high but narrowly compressed body covered with backward pointing spines. Both characteristics help them move forward easily between the hairs of animals or humans. When in the open they can leap with great agility and unpredictability, so that they are hard to catch. They are also difficult to crush because they are already so thin.

Most fleas are host-specific, living on only one species of host animal. Those in the family that contain the human, dog, cat, rat, and other rodent fleas are less rigidly so. This fact is important to man because fleas can carry disease. Rat and ground squirrel fleas can carry bubonic plague, also known as the Black Death.

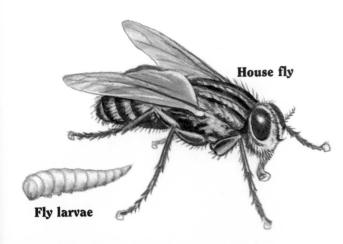

House fly

Fly larvae

FLY, HOUSE (arob, zebub); *Musca domestica.* L 1/4″

  GNAT (ken, kinnam) (konops).

  WORM; MAGGOT; (tola'ath, tola'ah, tola, rimmah, sas) (skolex).

The fourth plague the Lord sent to the Egyptians consisted of swarms of flies. It was the first one that did not involve the Israelites. That in itself was a miracle, considering that they kept herds of cattle, and cow manure is one of the choice environments for fly larvae to grow in. Also, even in normal times the number of flies in Egypt and other Middle Eastern countries is almost at plague proportions. The Philistines even had a "Lord of Flies," Beelzebub.

Travelers who visited those countries in the 1800s armed themselves with numerous concoctions to ward off flies, but nothing helped much. Instead they had to learn from the natives just to patiently endure them. Flies swarm in such abundance that one eats flies, breathes flies, and drinks flies. Crawling on one's face, they get into the mouth, nose, and eyes. The insects cover any unprotected food—they are eager to taste everything first. One has to shoo them off the food before eating. They swim in the traveler's drink and he has to strain them out.

The word fly brings to mind the common housefly, a most abundant creature in Palestine. It must certainly have been an important part of the swarms that entered the house of Pharaoh and his servants, and "corrupted" the land. They are still a real pest in some undeveloped, stock-raising lands. Who has not seen them crawl over the faces of starving children pictured on our television screens?

When the frogs that caused the second plague in Egypt died, the people gathered them in heaps, so "the land stank." Such mounds of decomposing bodies were an ideal place for flies to lay their eggs and have them hatch into maggots. Then flies swarmed over all the land. It was a natural sequence.

When God gave the children of Israel manna in the wilderness, He told them to gather no more than they could eat in a day, and not to try to keep it over for the next day. "But some of them left it until the morning, and it bred worms, and stank" (Exodus 16:20). The worms were undoubtedly the maggots of flies. It was the general belief in earlier days that maggots came into being through spontaneous generation. Not till 1688 did the Italian biologist, Francesco Redi, prove that maggots would not generate in meat if one kept flies away from it. The later work of Louis Pasteur finally laid to rest the theory of spontaneous generation. Life comes only from life, and only God can create new life from inert matter.

Isaiah, in chapter 66:24, speaks of worms (maggots) feeding on corpses, "for their worm shall not die, neither shall their fire be quenched." Job, in his well-known statement in Job 19:26, also refers to maggots: "And though after my skin worms destroy this body, yet in my flesh shall I see God." In Job 24:20 he states, "The worm shall feed sweetly on him." Bible writers sought to emphasize the permanence of death by noting the presence of maggots and the destruction of the flesh. Maggots are, of course, the larval stage of flies, but they are the ones most often meant when the Scriptures mention worms.

In Acts 12:23, in a reference to Herod's death, we have an inversion of what seems to be the ordinary process. It reads "The angel of the Lord smote him, because he gave not God the glory: and he was eaten of worms, and gave up the ghost." Either this is an awkward translation, though most other versions follow it, or else the worms ate him, and he died in consequence. Maggots do not eat live flesh. It is possible that he died of heavy infestation of tapeworm, one of the roundworms such as trichina, or, possibly, the Guinea worm, which some think to be the fiery serpent of the Israelites. This parasite lives under the skin and may burrow internally and enter the heart, or it may cause severe and even fatal poisoning. It infests a number of tropical countries, including Palestine.

The term *worm* also appears in the Bible in a derogatory sense of our being worms, that is, worthless or insignificant when compared to God (see Job 25:6; Psalm 22:6; and Isaiah 41:14). Here the Bible writer has no specific worm in mind. It is interesting to note that it is unlikely that he is thinking of the common earthworm. Earthworms prefer a damp, rich soil and were probably not that widespread in Palestine at the time.

Houseflies are an irritation and a nuisance, but at least they do not bite. The same applies to blowflies and fruit flies, but they spread disease, carrying infection on their feet, which they get into the food on our tables. There were, however, many other flies in Egypt that could have made the swarms a real trial to the people of the land.

The number of species of flies in the world is legion, and many of them inhabit the Holy Land. Among the so-called "biting" flies were the black flies, stable flies, horseflies, camel flies, sand flies, and mosquitoes. A dense swarm of black flies entering the palace of the pharaoh could have been a real threat to him. They are tenacious, and their bites swell into large welts. Horseflies and camel flies were a severe trial not only to the livestock but also to the people themselves. Sand flies, though small, come in large numbers, and their bites are as bad as those of mosquitoes, or worse. They may be the ones referred to in the Bible as gnats. Matthew 23:24 tells us not to strain out a gnat and swallow a camel. During fly season in Palestine, travelers have informed us in the past, it was sometimes necessary to place a loosely woven linen cloth over a mug when drinking to strain out the gnats and flies that landed there.

"Dead flies cause the ointment of the apothecary to send forth a stinking savour." Ecclesiastes 10:1 gives us an interesting little sidelight on life in Bible times. In those days ointments did not have a Vaseline base as they do now, but one of animal fats, which naturally draw flies. The flies tasting the ointment got stuck and died, and the druggist's customers did not appreciate the idea of "a fly in the ointment." In the same way a little folly in the life of a good man can spoil his reputation for integrity.

Mosquitoes were not common in most of the dry areas of Palestine, but the swampy districts near Beth Shan and the Hula Valley had plenty of them. They acted as agents in spreading malaria and yellow fever, and, because of that, some areas were at one time practically uninhabitable. In 1920 the Jewish settlers averaged two attacks of malaria a year in some localities. Now Israel has entirely eradicated the anopheles mosquito, and the land is free of malaria.

HORNET (sirah); *Vespa crabro.* L 1"

Hornets are common in the Holy Land, and Scripture most frequently mentions them for their fiery stings. In Exodus 23:27, 28 the Lord promised to send them ahead of His people to drive the Hivite, Canaanite, and the Hittite out of the land. Again in Deuteronomy 7:20 He says, "I will send the hornet among them, until they that are left . . . hide themselves." In Joshua 24:12 the old warrior recalls how the Lord figuratively did that.

It seems that hornets were so plentiful in some regions in Palestine that one place even received its name from them. *Zoreah*, mentioned in Joshua 15:33, means "the place of hornets."

Like bees, hornets are social insects, and build nests that have combs of cells, but they make them of their own manufacture of paper instead of wax. Several species of hornets inhabit Palestine. The big black ones build large paper globes suspended from tree branches. The smaller Oriental wasp makes uncovered paper combs, hung on the twigs of bushes. Some nest in holes or cracks in boulders, or in the ground. Wasps usually feed on insects or fruit juices, but some also raid beehives for honey. When a honey bee stings, it dies, for the stinger apparatus gets pulled out of its body. But a hornet can attack many times because its stinger does not have barbs like those of the bee. Sometimes the smaller wasps have stings even more painful than those of the larger ones. They are not ordinarily fatal except to individuals allergic to them.

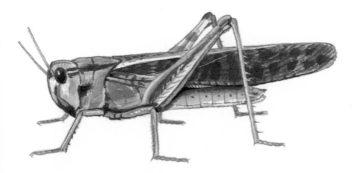

LOCUST, DESERT (arbeh); *Schistocerca gregaria.* L 2 1/2"

LOCUST, LEAPING (chargol); *Tettigonia vividissima.* L 2 1/2"

LOCUST, MIGRATORY; bald locust (sal'am); *Locusta migratoria.* L 2 1/2"

LOCUST, MOROCCAN; grasshopper (chagab); *Dociostaurus maroccanus.* L 2 1/4"

   CANKERWORM (yeleq).

   CATERPILLAR (chasil, yeleq).

   CRICKET (chargol).

   PALMERWORM (gazam).

The locust, or grasshopper, was an important insect to the Jews, a fact demonstrated by the use of 10 different Hebrew terms and one Greek in the Scriptures to denote it. The listing of clean meats in Leviticus 11:22 specifically cites four kinds.

The terms locust and grasshopper are not definitive, but are used somewhat interchangeably for the same species of insects. In Europe the larger ones usually are called locusts and the smaller ones are grasshoppers, but in America either term may apply to any member of the family Acrididae in the order Orthoptera. The linguistic problem here is that many people also refer to the cicada as a *locust*. We speak of the 17-year locust when we should say periodic cicada.

Locusts in the adult stage usually have two sets of wings. The front ones are hard, stiffly ribbed cases, while the back ones consist of thin, transparent tissue, folding neatly under the front covers when not in use and opening wide in flight. Locusts can make a loud, cracking sound in flight, either by rubbing their forelegs against the front wing covers or by scraping the edges of the front and back wings together. The various species have characteristic ways of doing it, and individuals all make slightly different sounds. They can hear each other by means of a sounding area on the back part of the thorax. After mating, the females lay packs of eggs in holes they dig in the dry earth. The eggs hatch the next spring, and the young go through several moults before they reach adulthood and get their flying wings.

The Hebrew term *arbeh* is the one most frequently used for "locust" in the Scriptures, and many believe it refers to the adult stage of the desert locust. The KJV has translated it as "locust" 20 times and as "grasshopper" four times. The desert locust swarms up from the Sudan, in Africa, about every 30 years. It is the one that has caused the greatest devastation in the Holy Land. During the tenth plague in Egypt (Exodus 10:4-19) a scourge of the insects devoured every "green thing." When locusts fly, they have little control over direction, and the wind carries them this way and that. An east wind brought them to Egypt, and then later, at the command of Moses, a west wind came and blew them all into the Red Sea.

Scholars believe that the biblical writers designated the migratory, or bald locust, by the Hebrew word *solam*. It is one listed in Leviticus 11:22 as clean and fit to eat. This locust has a wide range from Africa through Asia and even down to Australia.

Another species listed in the Levitical code as clean is the *chargol*, or leaping locust. *Chargol* sometimes gets translated as cricket and also as beetle, but generally scholars think it is one of the short-winged species, or wingless stages, ones that hop instead of fly.

Scripture also lists the *chagab* as edible. Usually translators render the term as "grasshopper," and some think it is the Moroccan locust, a smaller species often called "grasshopper." The word appears in Numbers 13:33, where the 10 spies said of the inhabitants of Canaan, "we were in our own sight as grasshoppers." And in Isaiah 40:22, where the prophet describes the inhabitants of the earth as being as grasshoppers.

The Hebrew term *gazam*, translated as "palmerworm" as well as "locust," may also refer to the immature stage of the migratory locust. At this wingless stage the locusts cannot travel rapidly, but they can still do considerable damage. Translators interpret *yeleq* as "caterpillar," "canker-worm," and "hopping locust." Again we may have the immature stage of either the migratory or desert locust rather than another species, or even an unrelated insect. *Geb* appears only once (Isaiah 33:4), where it refers to "the running to and fro of locusts." It is probably another word for the migratory locust. The term *selasal*, rendered as "locust" in the one place where it appears, may designate the cricket rather than the locust. *Gobay* and *gob* may possibly refer to swarms of locusts as a collective term, and *chasil* may mean the caterpillar, although it has been translated as "destroying locust."

Many other species of locusts exist in Palestine besides the ones we have tried to define. One notable one, not even referred to, is the giant grasshopper, *Saga ephippigera*, that grows to be seven inches long at times. Fortunately it eats insects and does the crops no harm.

As we have noticed from the biblical references, locusts often come in swarms, dense masses that blanket the fields and devour every green thing. We read in Proverbs 30:27 that they go "forth all of them by bands." One locust swarm in East Africa was 100 feet deep on a front one mile wide. It took nine hours to pass a point at a speed of about six miles an hour. Another swarm, near the Red Sea in 1889, is believed to have covered an area 2,000 miles square. Still another swarm that began in Algeria appeared in southern England after a journey of 2,000 miles. Some remnants of swarms have shown up 1,200 miles out to sea. Dense swarms may shut out the sun, greatly reduce visibility, and make the roads so slippery as to stop travel.

In the American west we have had great locust plagues in the 1870s, 1880s, and the "Dirty Thirties" that destroyed millions of dollars' worth of crops and discouraged many settlers as they attempted to establish homes on the prairies. Fortunately fall cultivation of egg-laying areas, the use of poison bait, and a number of other measures have helped to bring such devastating outbreaks under control.

In the 1920s scientists discovered that each of the migratory species of locusts also has a solitary group—some members of the species that do not migrate, but stay in one location. They seem to be more sluggish and to take on the color of their surroundings. (I have seen ones on the black cinders of a railway bed that were almost black, while others a few yards away, on light-colored soil and dry grass, were a lightly blotched tan in color.) Members of the gregarious phase have a more fixed pattern of strong black and yellow. Locusts have a high rate of metabolism that makes them highly active.

When overcrowded, the enlarged populations of the migratory phase break out and swarm to new territories, flying wherever the wind takes them, doing considerable damage, and eventually destroying themselves, or at least greatly reducing their numbers.

It is interesting to note that the Levitical code classifies locusts as clean food, fit to be eaten. Repulsive as it may seem to us, many of the desert people have used and still do use them as food. It is, when you come to think of it, understandable that when the voracious pests have destroyed crops and the people have nothing left to eat, they should turn to the marauders for food.

Desert nights are often cold and render the insects inactive. In the morning the Arabs throw their cloaks over swarms of semidormant locusts on the ground and bag them for breakfast. W. G. Palgrave, in his book *Central and Eastern Arabia*, tells of how excited his Arab companions were to find patches of locusts in the sand. They caught them, plucked off their heads, legs, and wings, roasted them over the fire, and ate them with relish. Some also eat them raw while holding them by their hind legs. Westerners who have eaten them say they are good, but we also hear that their flavor depends not only on how one prepares them, but on what they have been feeding.

When locusts swarm or there are far more than desert dwellers can eat at a meal, they dry them, grind them into a powder, and keep the insect flour for future use. Although likely to be bitter, when mixed with milk or honey, it is quite palatable.

We read in Matthew 3:4 and Mark 1:6 that John the Baptist lived in the desert and ate locusts and wild honey. Such fare was the normal food of people who lived in wilderness areas, and it was natural that he would have adopted it. Some believe that he lived on the beans of the locust, or carob, tree. While it might be possible, there is no need to explain away a food sanctioned by the Levitical code, just because it seems repulsive to us. It is likely that he ate what he could get and was not too choosy about it.

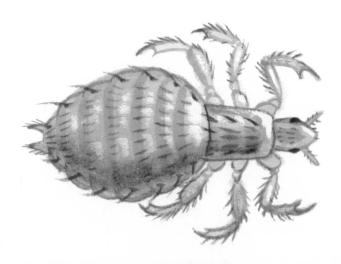

LOUSE, BODY (ken, kinnam); *Pediculus corporis.* L 1/30″

After the Lord sent the first two plagues to the Egyptians and the magicians managed, after a fashion, to duplicate them, He told Moses to strike the dust with his rod and turn it into a plague of lice that would infest both man and beast (Exodus 8:16-18). The magician-priests apparently could not duplicate or even avoid the infestation. As a matter of fact, they perhaps suffered from it in a way that others did not. In a country and time when all, from the beggar on the streets to the pharaoh on the throne, suffered from flies, fleas, lice, and other parasites, the priests took special care to avoid such pollution. They shaved their whole bodies and washed their clothing frequently to avoid harboring a single parasite. Now, if the plague was lice, they became so abundant that the priests could not possibly escape them. And since they were contaminated, they could not occupy any religious office or perform any religious rite. All pagan worship had to cease.

The KJV translates *kinnam* as "lice," and we will first consider them. Other versions also render it as "gnats," "maggots," "mosquitoes," and "ticks," indicating some disagreement as to just what the author originally intended.

Lice are small, white, dandruff-sized, wingless insects with a horizontally flattened body supported by six stout legs. Unlike fleas, they cannot hop, but crawl instead. They not only live on a specific host, but some of them even restrict themselves to certain parts of the body, as is true of the three main ones that parasitize man. The head louse inhabits the hair of the head, the body louse lives in the clothing and feeds on the body, and the crab louse infests the pubic hair and the armpits.

Specific ones live on horses, cattle, sheep, dogs, cats, and many other animals. Sucking lice feed upon the blood of their hosts. The numerous species of biting lice generally live on birds.

Some readers may have had experience with head lice as children in school. The insects will appear occasionally even in today's highly sanitary institutions. In the old days when some in the classroom caught them, we all had to wash our hair with kerosene and comb it with a fine-toothed comb to make sure we had none or to get rid of the ones we had picked up. Today's insecticides are more effective and certainly less smelly than the kerosene we used. Birds find dust baths helpful in controlling lice, but they would probably welcome insecticidal powder too. How the Egyptians coped with them, or whether they did at all, we have no record.

All lice, especially body lice, thrive under unsanitary conditions. They were rampant in the trenches during World War I to the extent that the soldier's parody of "Tramp, tramp, tramp, the boys are marching" as "Scratch, scratch, scratch, the lice are biting" became a popular refrain. One can control body lice by ordinary cleanliness, showers, and frequent laundering of clothes. Lice are not only a source of irritation and loss of blood, but they transmit a number of diseases, including typhus, trench fever, and relapsing fever.

Crab lice receive their name because their bodies are even broader than the others and the legs come out around the edge like those of a crab. They too thrive under unsanitary conditions, and people usually acquire them through sexual contact. Mercurial ointments or insecticides will destroy them.

An alternative translation of the Hebrew *kinnam* as "tick" has some merit in logic. As we have noted, lice cannot live well in dust, but ticks thrive in that element. God instructed Moses to strike the dust with his rod, and the dust turned to lice (or possibly ticks). Ticks are also flat like crab lice, but larger, nearly 1/4 inch long, and eight-legged. They are not insects, and are closely related to the spiders. Sucking blood from their hosts, they swell to more than double their size. Also they transmit disease. In many parts of the Near East the dust, around cattle wallows particularly, crawls with ticks. When cattle lie in it, they become infested, or exchange breeds. I have seen range horses reduced to skin and bones even when feed was good, because as many as a dozen blood sucking ticks per square inch covered their bodies. After being sweated under a horse blanket and given tick medicine they soon recovered and fattened up. Ticks will also attach themselves to man, and in the United States they can transmit the sometimes fatal Rocky Mountain spotted fever and Lyme disease.

MAGGOT—see Fly

MOSQUITO—see Fly

MOTH, CLOTHES (ash) (ses, sas); *Tineola bisselliela.* L 1/4"

Both the Old and New Testaments refer to the moth a number of times. Almost always that the writer had in mind the clothes moth and its destructiveness to clothing. We may think we are a clothes conscious people, and no doubt we are; but so were the ancients, especially the rich. The poor were lucky to have one coarse garment and a cloak. Since they wore them all the time, they did not need to worry about moths getting into them.

The wealthy, however, had great concern. They spent money on clothes not only to wear and impress people but also to give to honored guests and friends. In the parable of the wedding garment the host provided all his guests with wedding clothes, and he felt offended when one guest chose not to wear them. It was as if at a wedding today one of the attendants refused to wear a matching tuxedo that the groom had provided.

It was bestowing a great honor for a man to give his own clothes to another, especially if they carried with them the significance of office. Pharaoh dressed Joseph in "vestures of fine linen" (Genesis 41:42). Mordecai, "whom the king delighteth to honor," found himself arrayed in royal apparel, placed on the king's horse, and led down the street (Esther 6:8-11).

Clothes in those days required many days of weaving after the spinning of the wool. Then someone had to put in hours of hand sewing and decorating. Altogether each robe represented many days of skilled labor and artistry. People kept such garments in chests in special rooms, and royalty or the wealthy would assign a keeper of robes the duty of looking after them. He had to see to it that they were clean, in good repair, and especially that moths did not get at them.

Christ, in His sermon on the mount, warned His hearers, "Lay not up for yourselves treasures upon earth, where moth and rust doth corrupt, and where thieves break through and steal: but lay up for yourselves treasures in heaven, where neither moth nor rust doth corrupt" (Matthew 6:19, 20). Also in Luke 12:33 we read, "Sell that ye have, and give alms, provide yourselves bags which wax not old, a treasure in the heavens that faileth not, where no thief approacheth, neither moth corrupteth."

Three species of clothes moths have followed civilized man all over the world. The commonest of them is the naked clothes moth, so named because it does not make for itself a case, or gallery, out of the material it feeds on, tied together with its own silk, as do the other two. It does, however, spin a cocoon when it is ready to pupate. There is no point in killing the moths that fly up from stored clothing, for they have already laid their eggs. They are not the ones that chew the clothing. Rather the caterpillars that hatch from their eggs do the damage. One can destroy them by drycleaning, insecticides, or sunlight.

Moths no longer pose as great a problem as they did in earlier times, for synthetic fibers are not as attractive to the larva as woolen clothing. The cleanliness of the modern housewife, manifested in laundering and dry-cleaning fabrics, or in storing them in mothproof bags or chests, also greatly discourages their activities. Another factor that reduces the threat of moths is that clothes go out of style almost before the larva get a chance to chew them full of holes.

MOTH, SILKWORM (meshi) (serikon); *Bombyx mori.* L 2″

The word *silk* occurs several times in the KJV, but scholars are not sure that it is always correctly translated. In some cases they believe it should have been "fine linen." The last reference in the Bible (Revelation 18:12) does, however, accurately refer to silk, for the passage also lists fine linen with it. Without doubt, though, the Hebrews, since the time of Solomon at least, knew about silk. It is also certain that they were ignorant of its origin or manufacture.

The adult of the silkworm is a large, white moth, about two inches across. It lays from 300 to 500 eggs that hatch into silkworms, or more correctly caterpillars. They feed ravenously on fresh mulberry leaves supplied to them every few hours. After about four or five weeks they have grown to be three inches long and are quite fat. They crawl into little wooden cubicles provided for them, spin cocoons around themselves with fine two-stranded threads, and enter the pupa stage of their life cycle. The silkmakers then heat the cocoons to kill the silkworms, and soak them in warm water. Unraveling the silk, they spin it into threads, weave it into cloth, and dye it.

The manufacture of silk began in China but remained a secret for 3,000 years. The Persians bought the beautiful silks from the Chinese, established trade routes, and brought their wares to Damascus, the western distribution center for the Middle East and Europe. Eventually, about A.D. 550, two monks went to China, learned the secret of the manufacture of silk, and, at great risk to their lives, came back not only with the knowledge but also with some silkworm eggs and mulberry seeds they had managed to smuggle out in hollow canes. Then Italy became the western center for the manufacture of silk, and soon many other countries also produced it, including Lebanon, where it has since flourished.

Revelation 18:12 describes spiritual Babylon as a mythical entity, and, in highly poetic language lists many of the important trade items that were evidently the stock in trade of the merchants of the time. Silk is one of them. The wealthy Babylonians luxuriated in all the costly wares of the merchants, the "merchandise of gold, and silver, and precious stones, and of pearls, and fine linen, and purple, and silk, and scarlet."

PALMERWORM—see Locust

SCARLET—see Crimson Worm

SILK—see Moth, Silkworm

TICK—see Louse

WEEVIL, VINE; borer, vine (towla); *Cochylis ambiguella.* L 1/2"

Jonah 4:7 tells of a worm that God prepared, or appointed, to destroy the vine that had grown miraculously to shelter Jonah from the hot sun. We cannot be sure, but it was likely a species of vine weevil, or borer, that made the prophet so unhappy. The many different kinds of weevils live mostly on specific hosts. In the adult stage they are beetles with long snouts equipped with a drilling apparatus. The beetles drill holes in the stems or fruits of their hosts to lay their eggs in. The eggs hatch into larva, or worms, that eat out the inside of the plant. In some cases, as happened with Jonah's gourd, they kill it. The same thing may have happened to your summer squash in the garden. Of course, since the gourd in Jonah's case grew in a day and died the next day, either God greatly speeded up the natural processes or else both the gourd and the worm were special creations made for the purpose of teaching Jonah something of the value of a soul in God's sight.

Other Invertebrates

BLUE—see Murex

CORAL, RED (ramoth, peninim); *Corallium nobile.*

The Authorized Version translates the Hebrew *ramoth* as "coral," but the meaning is still uncertain. The same version renders *peninim* as "rubies," but others give it as "coral."

Traders sold polished objects made of red coral from the Mediterranean and Red Seas to the Israelites as gemstones, and it is quite possible that this is the substance intended in the passages. It was cut and polished, and though not rare was really quite attractive.

Many different kinds of coral grow in tropical seas. Like sponges, corals are colonial animals. Beginning life as free-swimming organisms, they then attach themselves to a solid base and start multiplying. By absorbing lime from the surrounding water, they build up a predetermined structure that varies according to the species. Enormous masses of coral, miles thick in places, have formed along continental shelves or as reefs surrounding islands.

In Job 28:18 we read regarding wisdom, "No mention shall be made of coral, or of pearls: for the price of wisdom is above rubies." Later, in Ezekiel 27:16, the word of the Lord declares, "Syria was thy merchant . . . they occupied thy fairs with emeralds, purple and broidered work, and fine linen, and coral, and agate." The following texts contain *peninim,* sometimes translated as "coral": Prov. 8:11, "For wisdom is better than rubies [coral];" (Prov. 8:11); "There is gold, and a multitude of rubies [coral]" (Prov. 20:15); "[A virtuous woman's] price is far above rubies [coral]"(Prov. 31:10); "Her Nazarites were . . . more ruddy in body than rubies [coral]" (Lam. 4:7). All of them would also fit the alternate translation of coral. If that is the case, coral may have been a rather common gem among the Jews.

HORSELEECH (aluqah); *Limnatus nilotica.* L 8″

In Proverbs 30:15 we read, "The horseleach hath two daughters, crying, Give, give." The passage refers to people who always want more and are never satisfied, just as the horseleech sucks, and sucks, and bloats, and still seeks more.

Leeches are members of the same phylum as the earthworms, and they are worms, but most of them live in water instead of in the soil. They are parasitic, as a rule, attaching themselves to fish and other vertebrates, including people, and absorbing blood till they have swollen to several times their original size. We may remember pulling them off our legs when swimming in freshwater ponds.

Physicians used medicinal leeches for ages to draw blood from patients they thought had an oversupply. That is the reason that people sometimes referred to doctors as "leeches."

The horseleech of the Middle East earned its name because it often lives in springs, wells, or horse troughs. When an animal comes to drink, the leech attaches itself to the inside of the mouth or nostrils and sucks till it bloats. Sometimes it clogs the nostrils, sinus cavities, and throat to the extent that it is not only painful and difficult for the animal to breathe, but the victim may die if the leech is not removed.

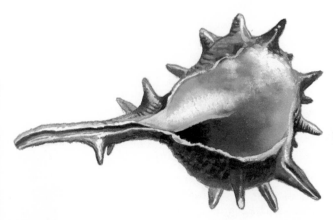

MUREX, DYE (argaman) (porphurous, porphura); *Murex brandaris*. L 3"

BLUE; PURPLE; SCARLET

Both the Old and New Testaments refer to purple, usually in connection with the tabernacle, Temple, or royalty. In ordinary practice today it is the secondary color made by mixing blue and red. But in biblical usage the term *purple* was usually nearer to red in the color spectrum, and it could range all the way to red. In fact, Scripture often uses "scarlet" interchangeably with "purple," as we will see from the texts quoted.

Purple was the ancient royal color of Babylon. "Whosoever shall read this writing, and shew me the interpretation thereof, shall be clothed in scarlet ["purple," margin], and have a chain of gold about his neck, and shall be the third ruler in the kingdom" (Daniel 5:7). The same applied to Medo-Persia. "And Mordecai went out from the presence of the king in royal apparel of blue ["violet," margin] and white, and a great crown of gold, and with a garment of fine linen and purple" (Esther 8:15). In Rome the consuls dressed in white robes with purple borders, but Caesar wore a purple toga. Anyone else wearing purple risked his life in doing so.

The deep maroon color was rich looking and attractive, but a big part of its value came from the difficulty in making it. The ancients manufactured purple from the contents of a shellfish known as the dye murex, or a similar one, *Murex trunculus*, both of which lived in the Mediterranean. These whelks prey on other shellfish, usually bivalves. Their rasping tongue wears through the shells and scrapes out the animal within.

Behind the head of the murex is a small capsule of yellow fluid—the dye. At one time the dyemakers cracked the shell with a small hammer, extracted the capsule, boiled it, and used the fluid as a dye. Judging from the large piles of broken shells around the harbor of Tyre, the ancient dyemakers apparently just crushed the shells in a large caldron, and boiled the mass to extract the dye. It is said that the smell of the boiling dye is much like that of rotting cabbage. The dye from one shell is only about enough to color an area the size of a dime, so it must have taken a lot of shells to dye one robe. Because the dye came from Tyre, it acquired the name royal tyrian purple. Though the liquid in the murex shell is yellow, exposing the dyed material to the sun changes its color to green, then blue and purple, and at last to the deep blood-red color of royalty. Extremely permanent, it becomes more beautiful with age.

The Scriptures tell us that the hangings of the tabernacle were of purple, the veil of the Temple was of blue and purple, and the high priest's garments also had purple in them. After the fall of Rome and the rise of the Catholic Church, the popes and cardinals also dressed in robes of purple and scarlet. Our purple today is no more expensive than any other color, but the symbolism remains to some extent. Today most of our dyes come from coal-tar products, and only shell collectors hunt the murex.

Lydia, we read in Acts 16:14, was "a seller of purple." Her purple, scholars tell us, came from the berries of the madder, *Rubia tinctorum*, that produced a red dye known as alizarin. Artists still use it as alizarin crimson, a brilliant, concentrated violet red color. We could also mention that the blue often used to dye royal garments had its origin in certain plants of the legume family, genus *Indigofera*, as well as the wood plant in the mustard family, and a few others. Crimson worm, a scale insect found on scrub oaks, provided the color crimson.

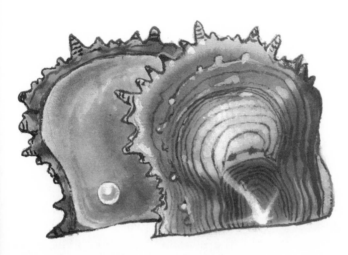

OYSTER, PEARL (gabish) (margarites); *Pinctada margaritifera.* L 6″

The pearl shows up only once in the Old Testament, but several times in the New. In Job's poetic answer on wisdom to his so-called friends (Job 28:18), he says, "No mention shall be made of coral, or of pearls: for the price of wisdom is above rubies." The Bible speaks of pearls in company with a number of other precious items: gold of Ophir, silver, onyx, sapphire, crystal, coral, rubies, and topaz. The others, with the exception of coral, are all minerals mined out of the earth. Coral and pearls grow in the sea from minerals that living organisms extract from the water. Pearls form when a grain of sand or other foreign matter enters the shell of an oyster, and certain cells produce a substance called nacre that coats the grain with layer upon layer of this lustrous substance to protect the oyster. Nacre is the same material as the mother of pearl that coats the inside of the shell, but the pearl, being separate from it, forms a sphere.

The Israelites would have found no pearls in Canaan, but merchant-men purchased them from traders who passed through there. Pearl fishermen worked both in the Persian Gulf and in the Red Sea, finding pearls there even in early times. They dived in the shallow water, and locating the oysters with their sensitive toes, they filled a net bag with them and came up. Usually they worked in pairs or groups from boats. A diver could stay under water for 50 to 80 seconds before having to surface for air. While there he had to be on the lookout for sharks, his only protection being a short knife. Needless to say, the lives of pearl divers were on the whole a bit shorter than the average, but the uncertainties of their existence added to the value of the pearls when they eventually reached the market.

Pearls sell by weight, but are valued according to their degree of perfection and their translucency. A flaw on the surface can devalue a pearl, but if it is to be strung the jeweler can drill the hole at the flaw. Sometimes one can peel off a flaw, reducing the size of the pearl but leaving it more valuable than before. (It seems that a good moralizer could draw a lesson from that somewhere.) The largest pearls are the size of golf balls. They occur in the giant oysters that grow in the South Pacific, but are not, however, very valuable. Dull white, they lack the luster of gem pearls—and, not many people want to wear pearls that size.

In Esther 1:16 the description of the furnishing of Ahasuerus' banquet hall employs the Hebrew word *dar*. The Revised Standard Version translates it as "mother of pearl." The substance is beautiful, but not as rare as real pearls, for it occurs in most shells. It provides material for backgrounds in mountings, for buttons, knife handles, and numerous other items.

Pearls are not always spherical. Sometimes they are flattened, and sometimes of irregular shape, especially those that have grown in abalones. Flattened pearls are not as valuable as spherical ones, but may be used in earrings. A well matched pair may still be worth quite a bit. Pearls strung on a necklace must all have the same size and color. They are not always white, but come in several tints, and may be pink, orange, gold, cream, or black. The latter are not really pitch-black, but a dark, lustrous gray, and are the most valuable of the colored ones.

The pearl of great price, mentioned in Matthew 13:45, 46, was so precious that the merchantman sold all he had to buy it. To be worth that much it would have had to be exceptionally large, perfectly spherical, translucent, iridescent, and flawless. Jesus compares it to the Kingdom of Heaven.

In the Sermon on the Mount, Jesus says, "Give not that which is holy unto the dogs, neither cast ye your pearls before swine, lest they trample them under their feet, and turn again and rend you" (Matthew 7:6). Commentators believe He had in mind the small seed pearls about the size of kernels of wheat or barley. While still quite valuable, they are of no use to swine. Christ apparently meant that it was not profitable to waste the precious words of the gospel on people who would only despise and ridicule them.

In 1 Timothy 2:9 Paul warns his protégé to discourage all outward adornment of "gold or pearls, or costly array" at the expense of character development. Revelation 17:4 and 18:12 and 16 portray the rich apparel, including pearls, of the woman on the scarlet beast who represented Babylon.

The last reference to pearls in the Bible (Revelation 21:21) describes the New Jerusalem, and states that the twelve gates will each be made of one pearl, hence the name "pearly gates." Probably it would be a mother-of-pearl type of surface, since it would be flat rather than spherical.

PURPLE—see Murex

SCARLET—see Murex

SCORPION, JUDEAN ('aqrab, scra'abin) (skorpios); *Buthus judaicus*. L 4"

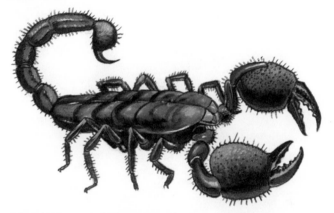

SCORPION, AFRICAN; *Androctonus australis.*

Scorpions are prolific in Palestine, and one has to be a little cautious where he sits if he does not want to get stung by one. The creatures like to hide in crevices in walls or under stones or boards during the day. (I have had the best success at finding them by turning over dried cow manure in the fields.) At night they come out of hiding and hunt around for spiders and insects to eat. At least 15 different species, ranging in size from one to six inches in length inhabit Palestine. They are a force to reckon with.

Scorpions are arachnids, in the same phylum as spiders, ticks, and king crabs. They have 12 segments in their abdomen, the back half of which forms the tail. This terminates in a hooked poison claw, and the scorpion can arch it over the back when in a threatening posture. Like others of its class, it has eight legs. Two additional front claws resemble those of a lobster, and it employs them for grasping and tearing apart its prey. The

119

sting of a scorpion is not deadly as a rule, but it is quite painful. Some claim to have gotten used to it after repeated stings. Maybe.

Most of the references in the Bible concern the scorpion's poisonous sting: "Who led thee through that great and terrible wilderness, wherein were fiery serpents, and scorpions" (Deut. 8:15), "Be not afraid of them, neither be afraid of their words, though briers and thorns be with thee, and thou dost dwell among scorpions" (Eze. 2:6). The latter passage compares the children of Israel themselves to scorpions.

When Jesus sent out His disciples, He said, "Behold, I give you power to tread on serpents and scorpions, . . . and nothing shall by any means hurt you" (Luke 10:19). In Luke 11:11, 12 Christ asks the parents among His hearers if a son of theirs should ask for bread, would they give him a stone, "or if he ask an egg, will he offer him a scorpion?" As we give good gifts to our children, so God gives good things to His.

In 2 Chronicles 10 and 1 Kings 12 we read of how the people came to Rehoboam, after Solomon's death, to ask if he would lighten the heavy burden of taxation his father had levied on them. On the advice of his young counselors, he rashly answered that as his father had chastised them with whips, "I will chastise you with scorpions." No wonder that most of the people decided to break away from Rehoboam and follow Jeroboam, thus causing the division of the land into Judah and Israel.

SNAIL (shabbelul); many genera and species.

Besides its listing as one of the unclean animals in Leviticus 11:30, the snail appears one other place in the Bible, Psalm 58:7, 8. Here David, in pronouncing curses on the wicked, says, "Let them melt away. . . . As a snail which melteth, let every one of them pass away."

It has been a common belief, also held among the Jews as borne out by the commentators on the Talmud, that snails melt in the sun. Actually a snail consists mostly of water and has little structure to it. When it dies and shrivels only a small grease spot remains, and thus it seems to have melted. People also used to believe that the trail it leaves was part of the snail, and that the farther it traveled the less there was of it, till it just disappeared. The trail is really mucus that the snail secretes. Actually snails feed on vegetable matter and grow rapidly larger, rather than smaller. They eat at night and hide in damp debris during the day.

Many species of snails live in the Holy Land. The one referred to in the Bible is probably one of the terrestrial varieties like the garden snail, that comes complete with a coiled shell on its back. Slugs are also snails, but just lack the shell. Most of the snails have a broad, muscular foot, a head region containing tentacles and eyes, and a mouth with a rasping tongue. The tongue enables them to scrape out and eat the pulp of strawberries, Swiss chard leaves, and other fruits and vegetables. The tentacles are soft, and the snail can withdraw them into themselves individually, and the whole creature can retreat completely into its shell.

Snails are gastropods, members of the mollusk phylum, which includes most living things with the kind of shells that hobbyists collect.

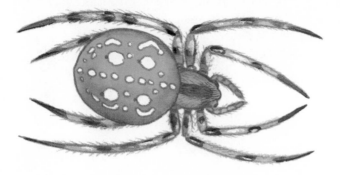

SPIDER ('akkabish, semamith); many genera and species.

Palestine is home to quite a number of the 20,000 different species of spiders known today. Orb spiders, like the garden spider, build a symmetrical web to catch their prey. Many other species also spin webs, nets, tunnels, etc., to trap insects. The balloon spider spins a long filament and sails out into the wind with it. The trapdoor spider hides in a hole in the ground and looks out from under a camouflaged trapdoor for its victim. When he sees one, he pops out, catches it, and drags it down to eat. The wolf spider builds no web, but stalks its prey, leaps on it, and kills it. The harvestman, or daddy longlegs, walks around on its long, spindly legs and eats when it happens to stumble on to an insect it can catch. Spiders eat a lot when they can, but when necessary they will go for weeks without eating—a convenient arrangement for a creature that has to wait for its meal to come to it.

Spiders are not insects, for they have eight legs instead of six. They belong to the same phylum as insects, but in a different class, Arachnida, which also includes the king crabs, scorpions, mites, and ticks.

In Job 8:14, 15 Bildad remonstrated with Job, saying that the patriarch had made the mistake of trusting in his integrity, "whose trust shall be a spider's web. He shall lean upon his house, but it shall not stand." He referred to the comparative flimsiness of the spider's web, that often needed repairs. The same thought also appears in Isaiah 59:5, 6: "They . . . weave the spider's web. . . . Their webs shall not become garments, neither shall they cover themselves with their works." It is interesting to note, though, that the filaments of the black widow's webs were strong enough to use as cross-hairs in the bomb sights of planes during World War II.

A text in the KJV is most intriguing to me because it is so true to the nature of spiders, but it is flawed in one respect. Proverbs 30:28 states, "The spider taketh hold with her hands, and is in king's palaces." One finds hardly a region on earth where spiders do not live. They range as far north and south as any insect life, and explorers have observed them on the high slopes of Mount Everest as well as under water. Spiders live in the humble shack of the peasant and also inhabit the palace of the king. They are a lesson in perseverance. "She taketh hold with her hands." The little creature has courage to tackle things. The only trouble with the text is that it is another example of mistranslation. The Hebrew word *semamith* should have been rendered "lizard" instead. It is so treated in most modern versions.

SPONGE, SHEEP'S WOOL (spoggos); *Hippiospongia lachne*.

The sponge receives mention in Matthew 27:48; Mark 15:36; and John 19:29. The three Synoptic accounts of the Crucifixion report how the Roman soldiers dipped a "spunge" into some vinegar (the acidic wine issued to the army) and offered it to Christ on the cross by means of a reed, after He had cried out, "My God, my God, why hast thou forsaken me?" The sponge was not one of our rubber or plastic ones, but was one of the untrimmed natural sponges that grow on the ocean floors.

For a long time people thought that sponges were plants, since they are stationary, do not respond to prodding, and do not seem to be predatory or to graze. Actually they are animals, feeding on the plankton that they draw in with the seawater.

Sponges exist in great variety. Some have glass spicules or calcium skeletons in them and are not useful to man, but the bath sponges— among which are the sheep's wool, glove, and grass sponge—are commercially in demand. The latter type of sponges are common in the Mediterranean, especially around the Greek Dodecanese Islands, and also along the coasts of Egypt. Most sponge divers, even in the United States, are of Greek origin.

Sponge divers, armed with hooked poles, dive into the coral waters, pull sponges loose when they see them, and haul them up into the boat in a wire basket. The sponges remain in the sun for a while so the animals inside rot. Then the fishermen beat, wash, and scrape them until they come out a clean golden yellow. The Roman soldiers in Christ's day must have brought their sponges with them from the Aegean. We still use natural sponges some today for car washing and in places where synthetic ones are not suitable.

Reptiles, Lizards

CHAMELEON (koach, tinshemeth); *Chamaeleo chamaeleon. L 14"*

Probably the most curious of all lizards in Palestine—and elsewhere—is the chameleon. It is an average-sized lizard with a long, prehensile tail that seems to have a mind of its own, or at least an eye on the end of it to enable it to know just where to grab a branch. The creature's feet have five toes and are prehensile, with some toes gripping one side of a branch and the rest the other side, making the animal extremely hard to dislodge. As it walks it deliberately sways backward and forward, imitating the action of a leaf in the breeze. The turret-shaped eyes can rotate individually to focus on its prey. The chameleon lives mainly on flies and small insects, and is an expert at catching them. When it spots a victim, it can shoot out a tongue longer than its body and, with the sticky substance on the end of it, ensnare its prey, and draw it with lightning speed back into its mouth.

The chameleon has an unusual ability to change the color of its skin. Although usually a yellow-green and brown, it can go through several changes when excited, or in reaction to its surroundings. It seems that the creature has no more power over its color transformations than a girl has over her blushes. The changes sometimes have an emotional basis, and sometimes result from a reaction to light. The lizard usually turns to the color of its surroundings, but not if they are red or blue. Against a red background, in one experiment, the animal turned black, then spots and rings of bright yellow appeared all over. Sometimes the color shifts continue even after death.

CROCODILE, NILE (liwyathan); *Crocodylus niloticus*. L 20'

The Hebrew word *liwyathan* occurs in three different references in the Scriptures. The KJV, as well as some other versions, records it as *leviathan* with no attempt to translate it to modern nomenclature. Other translations use the term crocodile for Job 41:1-33, and many scholars feel satisfied that it is the creature referred to in this graphic and imaginative poem.

The references in Psalm 74:14 and Isaiah 27:1, however, seem to indicate a mythical monster representing the source or cause of evil, a being elsewhere called Satan. Scripture says that God has broken its "heads." Canaanite mythology deals with a seven-headed monster called "leviathan." A cylinder seal from Tell Asmar in Mesopotamia shows heroes fighting a seven-headed dragon. The Bible also speaks of leviathan as a fleeing, twisting serpent. The text in Isaiah refers to the serpent of the "sea," or ocean. The saltwater crocodiles live mostly in salt marshes or estuaries and do not fit too well into the symbolism here. Isaiah may have had the whale in mind, but it is more likely that it was a mythical sea serpent.

The description in Job indicates that the author must have had a personal acquaintance with the creature and that it was not mythical, even though he uses some poetic license when he speaks of the flames issuing from his nostrils. He says, "His teeth are terrible round about." In *The New English Bible* we read from Job 41:15, "His back is row upon row of shields, enclosed in a wall of flints."

Throughout the world a number of crocodilians exist. Among them are the gavial and mugger of India, the cayman of South America, and the alligator of the southern United States. A saltwater crocodile, the largest of them all, lives along the coasts of southern Asia and Indonesia, and another one inhabits the tip of Florida and the West Indies. The rest of them, like our alligator, are freshwater species dwelling in rivers and marshes.

Fossil remains indicate that prehistoric crocodiles grew to be as long as 50 feet. The largest living specimens are seldom half that length, and most of them are a lot smaller. In spite of that, they are our largest living reptiles. One reason we do not find as many large ones around anymore is that over the world people have hunted them with high-powered rifles. Their decorative, scaled belly leather provides the raw material for expensive shoes and handbags. This militates against their longevity, and hence their greater size, for such reptiles continue to grow as they get older. Fortunately most countries now protect them, and the only legal skins now used come from reptile farms that raise them for that purpose.

The Nile crocodile was in ancient times common not only in the Nile but also in most of the rivers of Palestine. In the late 1800s an eight foot specimen was caught in the Kishon River, that flows through the Plain of Sharon. Now the crocodile is extinct in all that region including the Nile River below the Aswan Dam. In central Africa, however, many of them still live in the various rivers.

A female crocodile will lay from 20 to 90 eggs in a clutch. The eggs are a bit longer than hen's eggs, dirty white in color with thick, roughened, calcerous shells. The crocodile deposits them in holes that it digs in the river banks. There they hatch by the heat of the sun, but the mother remains nearby most of the time to guard them.

If all the eggs laid hatched and grew to maturity, crocodiles would overrun the world. Fortunately, this does not happen. The mother has numerous reasons to watch her eggs. Many predators, such as river turtles, monitor lizards, mongooses, jackals, and hyenas, keep alert for the—to them—delectable morsels.

When the female crocodile hears a faint hiccoughing sound, she knows that her young are ready to come out of the eggs, and she partly uncovers them. The young cut through the shell with a sharp "egg tooth" on the tips of their snouts that falls off later. Then they claw their way out of the shell and onto the sand, ready to face the world. Their first instinctive urge is to get to the nearest water.

On their way there hawks and vultures try to nab as many of the waddling nine-inch mouthfuls of food as they can. Those that reach the water find new dangers there. Fish, turtles, and other crocodiles wait for them. Then, if too many still survive, they turn on each other. The remaining ones swim away, hide, try to find food, and eventually grow up.

The adult crocodile is a creature well adapted to its environment. Ordinarily it lives on fish. It can swim rapidly with its muscular tail propelling it, but most fish can swim still faster. So it floats slowly like a log with only its nostrils above water. Then, when it finds itself near a fish or school of fish, it suddenly opens its jaws, sideswipes, slashes, and lunges after its prey with fair success. The crocodile's long rows of projecting teeth fit into depressions in the opposite jaws, allowing water to strain out without losing the fish. In its throat a fleshy valve back of its tongue closes out the water, and then allows the food to slip through.

The crocodile's sharp, irregular teeth do not work well for chewing, only for grasping and tearing. Should it seize a larger prey like a calf, sheep, or man, it holds it down under the water till it drowns, then drags it back to the bank to eat. There it grabs a leg and shakes the carcass with its powerful head and neck till a piece comes loose. In this way it may consume the whole carcass, or, if there is still too much, it will swim with the remainder to a hiding place and cover it with brush to finish at another time.

The jaw muscles of a crocodile are extremely powerful, as they need to be to tear apart a carcass or to hold an animal trying to free itself. The muscles that open the jaws, however, are surprisingly weak and a noose around the snout can render the jaws harmless. That is why alligator wrestlers can hold the reptile's mouth shut with just their bare hands.

Even the powerful crocodiles have enemies. Because of their eating habits, sluggish lifestyle, and the nature of tropical rivers, leeches and other parasites infest them. These pests attach themselves to the skin between the bony plates and in and around the mouth. As the reptile basks in the sun the crocodile bird (or zic-zac, as some have named it, after its call), a member of the plover family and related to the killdeer), comes along and picks off the leeches. Whether to accommodate the bird or to facilitate snoring, the crocodile often sleeps with its mouth open. The birds even enter the large mouth and pick out parasites and pieces of meat with apparently no danger to themselves. This symbiotic relationship seems to profit both and hurt neither. The bird's cries awaken the crocodile when danger threatens, and it slides off into the water and safety.

DRAGON (tannin) (drakon). L 30'

The term *dragon* appears a number of times in both the Old and the New Testaments. Invariably it is the symbol of evil. In all the Old Testament quotations (Psalm 74:13; Isaiah 27:1; 51:9; and Ezekiel 29:3-5; 32:2-8) it seems to refer to Pharaoh or the forces of evil as represented by the Philistines or other enemies of Israel. The two passages from Ezekiel describe the crocodile, which in turn could symbolize Egypt. When we come to the New Testament references in Revelation 12 and 20:2, John refers to Satan as the dragon with whom the early church found itself locked in deadly combat.

To Pliny and the early Greek writers, dragons were giant snakes, probably pythons, that lived in India and strangled their prey by constricting it in their coils. They were real creatures. The two serpents that crushed Laocoon and his two sons after they had warned the Trojans of the treachery that might lurk in the giant wooden horse the Greeks had built may have been symbolic of the Greek idea of a dragon.

A few centuries later, when explorers brought back from Java specimens of "flying" lizards, naturalists named them *Draco volans*, flying dragons. Of course, they were only about four inches long and did not fit in with the legends of great and terrible beasts. The still later discovery of the Komodo dragons on some of the Lesser Sunda Islands of Indonesia gave some substance to the myths about dragons, but they lacked wings.

Serious scientists also recognized that the animals were just larger editions of the monitor lizards known from a number of tropical countries. Also suggested as candidates for the dubious honor were the reported sightings of sea serpents supposedly seen in various bodies of water in central Africa, Scotland, and a number of oceans. Early maps depicted dragons in any watery regions not yet explored.

Dragons appear to have been central characters in many early legends. Hercules killed one; Beowulf slew Grendel; Saint George and Siegfried both killed dragons. Usually the dragons were enemies of the people, and the dragon slayers became folk heroes. In China, however, dragons were not necessarily evil. They lived in the sky and the people often looked upon them as symbols of royalty.

Early storytellers did not always agree on just how dragons looked, but all agreed that they were giant beasts and that they were terrible. When people found large prehistoric bones they decided that they must be the bones of dragons. Skulls of the woolly rhinoceros, a contemporary of the woolly mammoth, went on exhibition as those of dragons. Later discoveries of the bones of prehistoric pterodactyls or some of the dinosaurs might have given them more justification for their belief in dragons.

Usually people pictured dragons as reptilian, having four legs with clawed feet, leathery bat wings, a scaled body, a forked tongue, and breathing out fire from distended nostrils. When archaeologists excavated the Ishtar Gate in ancient Babylon, they found an alternating series of bulls and dragons done in blue tile decorating the walls on either side. They had scaled bodies, forked tongues, feet with eagle's claws, and long tails, but with horns on their foreheads and no wings. They must have represented the concept of dragons in Nebuchadnezzar's time. Perhaps it might have been the type of dragon Daniel killed in the apocryphal additions to the Old Testament book.

The visions recorded by the Bible prophets contain many composite beasts. Ezekiel saw four living creatures that mixed man, bird, and beast. Daniel witnessed in his dream a winged lion, a bear, a leopard with four wings, and a fourth beast that defied description, but was diverse from all others and "exceeding dreadful" (Daniel 7:19). It may have had some resemblance to the dragons of the Ishtar Gate.

In Revelation 12 John speaks of a great red dragon having seven heads, 10 horns, and seven crowns on those heads. Psalm 74:13 also mentions the "heads" of the dragons. Many-headed dragons, gods, and goddesses appear in other ancient religions. It seems doubtful that any such creatures actually lived (two-headed calves notwithstanding) even in those long-ago days. Rather they were the stuff of dreams, things seen in visions, products of the vivid imagination of the seers, created to symbolize the forces of evil in the world and Satan himself in his relation to the struggle of good against evil down through the eons of time.

GECKO, TURKISH (semamith, 'anaqah, leta'ah, chomet); *Tarentola mauritanica*. L 5″

Palestine currently has around 40 different species of lizards. Commentators believe that Leviticus 11:29, 30 refers to five or six different species, but we cannot be sure just which ones they are. Proverbs 30:28 speaks of the spider taking hold with her hands and being even in king's palaces. But the word *semamith* can also be translated as lizard, specifically the small house geckos abundant in Palestine.

Of these the Turkish gecko is the most common species in the Holy Land. This group of lizards gets its name from the call, "gecko-o," which they utter. Because of peculiar pads on their toes and their small size, they can not only walk on the walls of houses but can cling to the ceilings as well. Most householders tolerate them because they eat large numbers of flies and other insect pests that are much more of a nuisance.

LEVIATHAN—see Crocodile, Whale, Dragon

LIZARD, SYRIAN GREEN (leta'ah); *Lacerta trilineata.* L 15″

It is nearly impossible to untangle the web of translations of the Hebrew names of lizards, and we will not attempt to do so, but will just describe and picture some of the common ones in the Holy Land.

Most lizards in Palestine are rough-skinned, but the region also has a group of widely distributed soft-skinned lizards that vary widely in color to match their surroundings. One of the better known ones is the Syrian green lizard. As its color suggests, it lives in the remnants of green oak forests left in northern Palestine.

While the green lizard produces eggs that hatch by the heat of the sun, other lizards of the same genus that dwell in northern Europe bear their young alive. They keep the eggs inside their bodies till they hatch. In some cases we even find a difference within the same species, those living in the more northerly portion of their range being viviparous while those in the southern part lay eggs that hatch in the nest. Usually the mother watches over the eggs and even coils about them. This may be more of a protective gesture, for she would provide little body warmth.

LIZARD, THORN-TAILED; LIZARD, DABB; DHUBB (tzab); *Uromastix.* L 36"

The Middle East has a group of rough-scaled lizards, in the desert country of southern Palestine in particular, called *harduns*. Among them is the thorn-tailed lizard, also referred to as the dabb lizard, land crocodile, and crocodile of the desert. Its Arab name, *dhubb*, sounds somewhat like the Hebrew *tzab*, used in the passage in Leviticus 11:29, and some think it might be the one listed there as unclean. This large reptile sometimes grows to be three feet long. It reminds one of the gila monster of the American southwest, but the two are unrelated. Like the gila monster it has a heavy tail, but instead of having a covering of hard knobby armor, the dhubb's tail has on it whorls of sharp-edged scales. It serves as a good defensive weapon against its enemies.

In the cool of the morning the dhubb is gray in color and moves sluggishly, but as the sun warms it, the lizard becomes more brown, stands up on its stout legs, and can move around quite swiftly. It is not dangerous, however, for it is a vegetarian and lives on some of the succulent plants that grow in the desert.

The related ornate dabb lizard of the granite hill country and the Sinai agama are both more attractively colored, though not observed as often. Most common of the dabbs and most often seen because it lives in more settled localities is the starred agama of northern Palestine.

MONITOR, NILE (koach); *Varanus niloticus.* L 48″

The Nile monitor lizard, which sometimes grows to be up to six feet long, is even bigger than the thorn-tailed, but it is of more slender build and has a long, whiplike tail that makes up quite a bit of its length. This active reptile preys on other lizards, rats, and mice, and is quite fond of crocodile eggs, which it devours in large numbers when it finds them. The Arabs eat and relish both the Nile monitor and the land monitor (the latter is even more common in Palestine), and there would seem to be more reason to prohibit the eating of their flesh than that of the small, bony chameleon, also suggested for the Hebrew word *koach*.

Female monitors claw an opening in the live nest of a colony of termites and lay their eggs there. The termites quickly seal the opening again and maintain a relatively even temperature for the hatching eggs. Being vegetarians, the termites do not bother the eggs, which thus remain well hidden from predators. The young hatch and claw their way out of the nest when they are ready.

MONSTER, SEA—see Crocodile; Whale (Volume 1, Mammals)

SKINK, BRIDLED (leta'ah, chomet); *Chalcides ocellatus.* L 9″

Skinks are some of the most common lizards in the world, and a number of species inhabit the Holy Land. They are smooth, often striped, have small, weak legs, but a sinewy body that helps propel them like a snake. Their overlapping scales aid them in such locomotion. The bridled skink pictured in this volume is typical of the group as a whole. Another representative example is the golden Cypriot skink. Its yellowish body has orange and red dots, and it has curious ears toothed on the front side. The common skink lives in sandy areas and can rapidly bury itself.

Reptiles, Snakes

SNAKES (nachash, tannin, zachal) (ophis, herpeton). also Creeping Things

Today 35 different species of snakes live in Palestine. Seven of them are poisonous, but of them only one, the Palestinian viper, ranges into settled areas. Most of the others dwell in the desert.

Ever since the deception of Eve in the Garden of Eden, snakes have had a bad reputation. Humanity in general views them with prejudice and distrust. The Scriptures employ them as symbols of dishonesty, stealthiness, slander, evil, and cunning. Revelation 20:2 refers to Satan as "that old serpent." Elsewhere the Bible speaks of snakes as tools of God's wrath: "The Lord sent fiery serpents among them" (Numbers 21:6). Strong wine "biteth like a serpent, and stingeth like an adder" (Proverbs 23:32). Evil men "have sharpened their tongues like a serpent, adder's poison is under their lips" (Psalm 110:3). Or they "suck the poison of asps: the viper's tongue shall slay [them]" (Job 20:16).

On the other hand, Scripture uses them as symbols of wisdom: "Now the serpent was more subtil than any beast of the field" (Genesis 3:1). "Be ye therefore wise as serpents" (Matthew 10:16).

The Bible uses 10 Hebrew and four Greek words to denote snakes. Some, like those at the beginning of this section, just refer to snakes in general, while others seem to denote specific ones. Where possible, we will indicate the species suggested and the reasons for selecting it.

ADDER—see Cobra; Viper, Horned

ASP—see Cobra

COBRA, EGYPTIAN (pethan) (aspis); *Naja haje.* L 36"

Translators have rendered the Hebrew *pethan* as "asp" and "adder" in Deuteronomy 32:33; Job 20:14, 16; Psalm 58:4; 91:13; and Isaiah 11:8. The context seems to indicate a highly poisonous snake that people greatly feared. Scholars believe it to be the Egyptian cobra, found over much of the dry areas of eastern and northern Africa, and into Palestine. It is closely related to the Indian cobra, *Naja naja.*

Cobras have the unusual ability of spreading the upper part of the body into a hood when they assume a threatening posture. They can do so because the ribs in that part of the body are flat instead of curved, and, when relaxed, they lie back along the spine. When drawn forward, however, they spread the elastic skin of the "neck" into a hood usually ornamented with a formation of darkened scales on the back.

Cobras bring the idea of snake charmers to mind. The Bible also alludes to them several times. When Aaron threw his staff down before Pharaoh (Exodus 7:10) and it became a serpent, the Egyptian magicians did the same. Charmers, we are told, can render snakes rigid by applying pressure on the sides of the snake's neck. Some have suggested that the magicians fooled Pharaoh through such a technique.

Psalm 58:4, 5 speaks of the "deaf adder that stoppeth her ear; which will not hearken to the voice of charmers." Evidently snake charmers played to serpents even in David's time, as they still do today. Ecclesiastes 10:11 declares, "Surely the serpent will bite without enchantment." Jeremiah 8:17 says, "I will send serpents, cockatrices, among you, which will not be charmed, and they shall bite you, saith the Lord."

Herpetologists do not yet fully understand just how snake charmers accomplish their feats. Some say that they render the snakes harmless by breaking their fangs off, but the reptiles have several sets of fangs that come up successively to replace the damaged ones. Some charmers will even work with wild snakes at their dens, or with recently caught ones. A lot of their skill is in knowing their cobras well—what they will do and what they won't. However, charmers do get bitten occasionally.

The Egyptian cobra ranges from southern Palestine into Egypt and Africa. Its dull, satiny scales vary considerably, but the Palestinian specimens are usually blackish brown. Alert and irritable reptiles, they will rear, ready to strike, at the slightest provocation. The spitting cobra, a related species, inhabits northern Africa and part of the same range as the Egyptian. The large snake, it is said, has the ability to shoot venom out of its fangs and can accurately hit the eyes of a person eight feet away.

COCKATRIX—see Viper, Palestinian

SAND BOA, JAVELIN; *Eyrx jaculus.* L 28"

WATER SNAKE, DICED; *Natrix tessalatus.* L 42"

WHIP SNAKE, BLACK; *Coluber jugularis.* L 84"

It is interesting to note that of all the snakes found in Palestine, Scripture mentions only the poisonous ones in any specific way. There are also a number of nonpoisonous ones that we will consider briefly. The javelin sand boa is a small member of the constrictor family. It is less than 30 inches long and lives on insects and rodents. Like other sand boas, its head is so small that it resembles the blunted tail, and it is sometimes hard to tell one end from the other.

The diced water snake frequents streams, and it feeds on small fish. It is growing in numbers now because of the use of irrigation and the increased breeding of fish in artificial ponds. The word "diced" in its name refers to the pattern of markings on its slender body.

The black whip snake is the longest snake in the Holy Land. It has a small head, slender neck, and long tail that can add up to all of seven feet in length. Feeding on rodents, birds, and their eggs, it is an accomplished tree climber. All whip snakes are active and do not do well in captivity.

VIPER, CARPET—see Viper, Horned

The Hebrew word *shephiphon* appears only once in the Scriptures (Genesis 49:17), and the KJV translates it as "adder" and the RSV renders it "viper." Scholars usually understand the term to refer to the horned viper. Jacob, on his deathbed, in blessing his twelve sons, says, "Dan shall be a serpent by the way, an adder in the path, that biteth the horse heels, so that his rider shall fall backward." The patriarch's left-handed "blessing" describes the horned viper quite well. The marginal reading "horned snake" may refer to the triangular shape of the viper's head.

The horned viper is a highly poisonous snake abundant in North Africa, and it also occupies the sandy areas of southern Palestine. The two modified scales that form "horns" over the eyes make it readily identifiable. It is a heavy, rather slow reptile, and since it preys on the active jerboa and other desert rodents, it must catch them by stealth. The viper finds a depression in the sand, often a camel's or a horse's footprint, and with a few lateral movements of its flattened body, it buries itself in the sand. The reptile is nearly the color of the dust in which it lives, and the camouflage is thus quite good. Here it waits for a rat to come by.

Thus lurking in a camel's footprint, it often becomes "an adder in the path" of any unwary traveler. Being of an irritable nature and not seeing too well, the viper will often strike at the foot of a horse going by. Desert horses are aware of the vipers and fear them, but because the snakes are barely two feet long and well hidden in the sand, they have difficulty detecting them till they strike. Then the horse is likely to rear up and throw off his rider.

The fangs of the horned viper are long, hollow, and needlelike. Almost hidden by the fleshy covering and laid back along the roof of the mouth until the viper strikes, they then rise at right angles to the upper jaw. The large poison glands located at the sides of the jaws account for the exceptional width of the viper's triangular head. The horned viper is dreaded even more than the cobra because one cannot see it until it attacks.

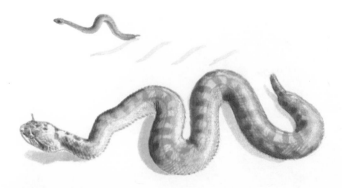

VIPER, HORNED (shephiphon, saraph meopheph, nachash saraph); *Cerastes cornutus.* L 30″

Because it lives in the sandy deserts, the ordinary form of snake locomotion—moving the belly scales by rib motion against any projections on the ground, or the weaving and pushing of its coils against vegetation, rocks, and brush—does not work, for the sand gives way everywhere. The horned viper lacks the wide locomotive scales on the belly that most other snakes possess. For those reasons it uses the same method of travel as does the sidewinder, a rattlesnake of the American southwestern deserts, throwing itself in coil after coil across the sand. Its flattened body pushes against the sand and it can move quite rapidly when necessary.

The KJV has "flying serpent" for the term *saraph me'opheph* in Isaiah 14:29 and 30:6. No real flying serpent with wings existed even in Bible times, but there is a flying snake in southern Asia and Indonesia that is able to flatten its body enough to soar from a higher branch to a lower one. However, this is probably not what the passage above meant by "flying serpent." More likely the author had in mind, the horned or the sand viper for they both appear to fly over the sand as they travel in their sidewinder motion. The "fiery" is not hard to understand, since it is an expression we often use ourselves when we speak of an intense pain. The poison of the vipers causes a severe burning pain.

The various Bible versions translate the Hebrew *akhhub* as "adder" and "viper." It is thought to be another species of viper, possibly the carpet viper. This snake is smaller than the horned or sand vipers, it has beautiful markings, as the name might indicate. The carpet viper occupies the same desert regions as the other two, but its habitat is not the sandy places. Instead it lives in the gravely, rocky areas, where its richly marked body blends better with the mottled reddish gravel and light-colored pebbles.

VIPER, PALESTINIAN (epheh, siphonin) (echidna); *Vipera palastinae*. L 48"

The Palestinian viper is one of the most dangerous snakes in the Holy Land, largely because it likes to live in the vicinity of houses and even in them, for it feeds on rats and mice. Another reason people have feared it so greatly is that until recently no antidote existed for its poison. Of course, that was true of all of snake venom in Bible times.

The two words *epheh* and *siphonia* appear in Proverbs 23:32; Isaiah 11:8; 14:29; 59:5; and Jeremiah 8:17. The Authorized Version renders them as "cockatrice" in Isaiah, with "adder" in the margin, and as "adder" in Proverbs. More recent versions refer to it as "adder." The text in Isaiah 11:8 speaks of a "weaned child" putting his hand on a cockatrice den, which would indicate proximity to a house. One recoils in horror at the thought of a child exposed to such a deadly snake, but the biblical writer uses the picture to contrast life on the present earth with that in the earth made new. In Isaiah 14:29 we read of the fruit of the cockatrice being a "fiery, flying serpent." That would seem to indicate the horned or sand vipers for reasons explained under the horned viper heading.

The New Testament employs the Greek word *echidna* five times and it is translated as "viper." Most of the references to it involve John the Baptist calling the scribes and Pharisees a "generation of vipers." The mention in Acts 28:3, however, tells of the viper that fastened itself to Paul's hand as he gathered wood for a fire after his shipwreck on an island in the Mediterranean. It could well have been the Palestinian viper, for it is common on all those coasts.

VIPER, SAND (epheh, nachash saraph); *Cerastes vipera*. L 24"

The word *'eph'eh* used in Job 20:16; Isaiah 30:6; and 59:5 usually appears as "viper" in English. Scripture describes it as a beast coming from the south, Egypt, that it lays eggs, and also that it is full of deadly poison. In the text in Job we find expressed in Zophar's speech an idea common among most early people, that the snake's poison resides in the forked tongue. The tongue, though colored red and black, and though it darts in and out in a sinister way, is nothing more than a sense organ that helps the snake to detect food and danger. It is possible that *epheh* represents the sand viper. This common desert viper resembles the horned viper in habits and appearance, but it lacks the "horns." Also, it is a sidewinder and inhabits the deserts of Palestine, Arabia, and Africa. An alternate possibility is the mole viper, a small, burrowing viper that is, however, long-fanged and extremely poisonous.

The Hebrew terms *nachash saraph,* used in Numbers 21:6 and Deuteronomy 8:15, have been translated as "fiery serpents." They were the snakes that caused such consternation among the Israelites during their journey through the Sinai Peninsula. Sand vipers were common there, and they were probably responsible for punishing the people for their murmurings. The term could have also included horned vipers.

God instructed Moses to make a replica of the serpents and raise it on a pole so that the people could demonstrate their faith by looking at it and be healed. Symbolically the image represented Christ, as He Himself later stated in John 3:14. (In Revelation 20:2, the serpent stood for Satan.) The Israelites soon forgot the significance of the brazen serpent. They took it to Canaan with them and worshiped it as an idol till the time of Hezekiah, who broke it in pieces (2 Kings 18:4).

Turtles

TORTOISE, MOORISH (tzab); *Tesudo graeca.* L 10″

Though mentioned in the Bible only once (Lev. 11:29) and translated in the KJV as "tortoise" (also as "great lizard" in other translations), the tortoise and turtle are common in the Holy Land, and we will discuss both of them. The above text forbids the reptiles as food, but local people other than Jews eat them and their eggs with relish.

The Moorish tortoise occupies most of the desert areas around the Mediterranean. About 10 inches long, it has a high-domed shell, stumplike legs, and extremely short tail. It is deliberate in all its movements. No doubt Aesop had the creature in mind when he told the fable about the hare and the tortoise. The story probably does not quite represent the creature's nature, however, for it is more likely than the hare to have been the one to rest a few hours after a little exertion. At the driest part of the year the tortoise will often dig itself into the sand and aestivate for a few weeks till rains come. During winter it also digs down below the frost line and hibernates through the cold months.

Its shell protects the tortoise from most of the smaller predators or birds of prey. The lammergeier, however, will grasp the shell, lift it to a great height, and drop it to some rocky ground, something not hard to find in that country. Then it feasts on the smashed remains.

Arabs hunt the slow creatures, boil their carcasses till the meat separates from the shell, and devour them. They also dig up the eggs and cook them to eat. The eggs are small, almost round, and have a thick, hard shell that has the texture of sandpaper.

In England people reserve the term tortoise for those shell-backed reptiles that live on land or in fresh water, their marine relatives being referred to as turtles. It is now more common to call only the strictly terrestrial ones tortoises and all the rest of them turtles. The American southwestern desert tortoise and the gopher tortoises of the southern United States are nearest in appearance and lifestyle to the Moorish tortoise.

TURTLE, RIVER; Caspian terrapin; *Clemmys caspica.* L 8″

The KJV uses the word *turtle* in the poetic verse in Song of Songs 2:12, "the voice of the turtle is heard in our land," but it is almost certain that the writer had turtle dove in mind. Turtles are practically voiceless. The river turtle is a common species in Palestine. It is smaller than the tortoise, only eight inches long including a well developed tail. In appearance it resembles the American chicken turtle more than any of the others. The legs are somewhat paddle-like and have webbed toes. The shell is olive colored with black and yellow markings on it.

River turtles live in most freshwater ponds and streams in Palestine. They are active swimmers and, unlike the vegetarian tortoises, are carnivorous, living largely on fish—dead or alive. The turtle will rise up slowly under a fish sunning itself near the surface of a pond and, like a pirhana, will take a bite out of the underside with its razor-sharp beak. The fish usually swims away, but soon dies; then the turtle finds it and finishes its meal. It can consume enormous quantities of food at a time, then go for days without eating.

The eggs of river turtles are more oval than those of the tortoise, and their shells are smooth, white, and porcelain-like. The females lay them in holes they dig in the riverbanks and then leave them to hatch in the warmth of the sun. Men and other predators hunt for the eggs and eat them whenever they find them, thus decreasing the danger of overpopulation.

Should the pond or stream in which they live dry up, as often happens in that country, the turtles will dig down and aestivate till the rains come again. In winter they also hibernate during the cold months.

In addition to the two members of the turtle family that we have mentioned, there is also a rare species of soft-shelled turtle, *Trionyx triunguis*, that now inhabits the rivers of Israel. Three species of sea turtles lay their eggs on the beaches of Palestine.

8